MW00328763

The Japan Leadership Series

Japan Business Mastery
What you *really* need to know

Dr Greg Story
President, Dale Carnegie Japan

Copyright © 2019 Dr Greg Story. All rights reserved.
ISBN: 978-4-909535-01-6

Dale Carnegie Training Japan
Tokyo
japan.dalecarnegie.com

FIRST EDITION
August 2019

Table of Contents

Introduction

J apan has dropped off the radar globally. The rise of China
has placed the nation in the shade. This is quite strange,
really, given that Japan is the world's third-largest economy,
has a vast capital surplus, a commitment to free trade, rule of
law, and is a sophisticated, high-tech nation that needs to import
a lot of goods and services. When people visit Japan, they are
impressed by the order, cleanliness, politeness, punctuality
of the transport system, and way in which everyone is so well
dressed and nicely presented.

One of the consequences of this reversal of prominence is
that there are relatively few business books on Japan being produced. My first book, *Japan Sales Mastery*, became a number-one
bestseller in its category on Amazon. If you are selling to Japanese
buyers, you will definitely find that this how-to book will spare you
a lot of pain. *Japan Sales Mastery* filled quite a small niche and so
was highly specialised in its scope. After releasing it, I realised that
there were no current books on doing business in Japan.

So, I decided to write this book on broader, more general
topics about the business basics you need to succeed in Japan.
This book is for those who deal with Japanese bosses or colleagues
in their home countries, for those business people who travel to
Japan, and for those living in Japan who may not be that familiar
with how things work around here.

I have been lucky to have worked in trade and to have dealt
with so many products and services. I also spent seven years in
retail banking here and now run a corporate training company.
The trade and training portfolios of industries and sectors covered
are immensely broad. This has allowed me a window into many
aspects of business in Japan, many more than if I had just been in
one industry such as banking.

I have selected themes for the book around the types of issues
which always come up for foreigners doing business with Japanese
people. I hope these topics prove useful and provide insight into

Japan as a market. I only wade into the territory of cultural differences where it is relevant to business. There are many other books which do a much better job of concentrating on that subject.

This is a book for businesspeople like me, who have struggled, been mystified, surprised, disappointed, and delighted by doing business here. I hope I have provided some insights. I hope I can elevate the chances of your being delighted, rather than the opposite alternatives I have listed. Japan is challenging; there is no doubt about that. When we have a better understanding of how things work here, we will do much better for our organisations and for ourselves. That is my sincere wish for you the readers, and so please enjoy *Japan Business Mastery*.

Dr Greg Story
President, Dale Carnegie Training Japan
greg.story@dalecarnegie.com
enjapan.dalecarnegie.com

Acknowledgments

J apan loomed large for me as an 11-year-old in Brisbane, Australia, sitting on the floor in front of the television watching *Onmitsu Kenshi*, also known as *The Samurai*. For a boy brought up on American cowboy shows for kids, samurai fighting with swords against ninja armed with star knives was like something from Mars. Like young people today, who discover an interest in Japan through manga and anime, I got hooked early through that television show. So, I should thank whoever it was who convinced an Australian commercial broadcaster to air this programme from Japan in 1964. It must have been a bold decision at the time.

I furthered my Japan addiction with the study of traditional Shitoryu karate beginning in 1971, in my hometown of Brisbane. I want to thank my Japanese karate teachers Kusano-sensei and Iba-sensei for baffling me. This was my first collision with Japanese cultural differences, and it was mindboggling at the time. If I thought something was up, they thought it was down. If I thought it was right, they thought it was left. I remember thinking, "What is going on here?" That puzzlement led me to want to go to Japan to understand how Japanese people thought, so I could master karate.

Dr John Welfield, my professor of Japanese politics in the Modern Asian Studies programme at Griffith University in South-East Queensland, was a fantastic teacher who was so knowledgeable about Japan. He was so inspiring. I decided to emulate him and also become a professor teaching international relations and Japanese politics.

That course of action led to a scholarship from Monbusho—at the time Japan's Ministry of Education, Science, Sports and Culture—to study in Tokyo at Jochi University, now better known as Sophia University.

Professor Michio Royama was a visiting professor at Griffith University, and his assistance in getting the scholarship was vital. A subsequent Master's Degree in Japan at Jochi—and then a PhD at Griffith University under the supervision of Professor Alan Rix, who was at the University of Queensland—started me on the path to an academic calling.

Japan's economic bubble of the late 1980s side-tracked me into business. Ian Mackie, at Jones Lang Wootton in Brisbane, was a great teacher of hard-edged business skills in the international real-estate world. The bubble burst, and I was fortunate to be hired by Greg Dodds, who was running Austrade—the Australian Trade and Investment Commission—in Japan. He hired me to come back to Japan to open a trade office in Nagoya. I worked for him throughout my later transfers to Osaka and Tokyo. Greg is someone who really knows Japan, and I learnt a lot from him.

Sajeeve Thomas hired me away from Austrade to join the Retail Bank at Shinsei. We were changing the world of retail banking over there, and it was very exciting to come up with an idea in the morning and be executing it in the afternoon. Through Korn Ferry's introduction, Leigh Watson headhunted me out of Shinsei Bank to run the National Australia Bank's Japanese operations, just in time to enjoy the full intensity of the Lehmann Shock and the meltdown of the financial sector. You learn a lot about Japan in adversity, I found.

I would like to thank my Japanese team at Dale Carnegie Training Japan for continuing to educate me about business in Japan. They are very good at applying some reality checks to their Aussie boss's shiny new ideas. The many hours required to write this book were devoted in my study at home—the door closed—to allow me to concentrate. I needed space and time. I am very appreciative to have such a supportive and understanding family who allowed me to complete this book.

Finally, I want to thank you, the reader, for your interest in business in Japan. Over the years, I have read many books and articles on the subject which have helped me understand this amazing country. I hope that my book does that for you.

1 — Trust

T rust is a big issue in Japan. The concept of trust in business here is a bit more complicated than in typical Western economies. The discussion goes beyond getting paid or not getting paid for goods and services, sticking by the agreement, doing what you promised, etc. The people we deal with in companies are salaried employees who have probably been with that company their whole career. They are primarily interested in gradually moving up internally by making no mistakes. The best way not to make a mistake is to do nothing new or risky.

Their aversion to risk precludes trying anything that might have a negative impact, even if that means denying the company business opportunities. Most Western companies are looking to reward risk-taking, but risk is seen quite differently in Japan. There is little reward here for risk-taking, and a big downside if things go wrong. So, when we approach a Japanese company, we have to think about how we can take away the risk for the individual with whom we are dealing. It might be through money-back guarantees, warranties, escape clauses, etc.

This attitude toward risk is summed up by the saying, "Japanese buyers prefer the devil they know to the angel they don't know". By definition, you are the angel they don't know, because you are offering a new product or service, or an alternative to what they are using now. They would rather go with a higher price and more certainty than to shave off a few yen while introducing a higher level of risk. Our "pricing advantage" doesn't resonate— especially when we have not been able to also resonate with the buyer's concerns about risk.

In the distribution system in Japan, there is a very complex food chain to work through. There are many layers, and if you don't deliver as you said you would—when you said you would—you endanger the whole interlocking food chain.

This is where the real trust comes into play, and it isn't just about discounts on price points. No Japanese company wants to

see their distribution system set on fire by a new player, someone
they don't really know well. This is why we also say, "Getting
business done takes a long time in Japan". Therefore, they are very
conservative about introducing a new supplier into their ecosys-
tem. This is a business marriage, not a one-night stand.

There are many examples where aggressive pricing doesn't
cut it and doesn't open the doors to deals. For example, when you
are competing in the marketplace with the big Japanese trading
companies, they take the risk away for their buyers by providing
very long payment terms. They will have set a higher price than
what you can probably supply for, but their offer is a lot less risky.
Their client company can land the product, sell it, and then pay the
trading company later. Your discounted price—though attrac-
tive—can't compete with that risk-free arrangement.

Because of the buyer's preponderance for risk aversion, due
diligence here is performed very carefully and usually very slowly.
Deals in Japan rarely get done in one meeting, so we must expect
multiple meetings. Things take a lot longer here because companies must gain consensus internally if they are to make a change to
their supply arrangements. Everyone is concerned about making
sure the risk component of a new supplier arrangement has been
removed before they will agree to move forward. It might take
years, in fact, before the buyer is comfortable with even giving you
a try. Remember, the individuals involved are rewarded for reducing risk rather than raising additional revenues.

This happens in my own training business here all the time.
Companies we met four years ago finally send one person to trial
the training. It can drive you nuts, but this is how it is—and if you
want to play, then you have to pay.

Western companies being driven by quarterly earnings and
the stock price have a hard time with Japanese long-play time
frames. Think risk-reduction strategies and also think long term
when dealing with buyers. Suggest trial orders, small-scale testing,
and low-risk activities, and show sustained quality and logistics
capability. If you can approach the sales process this way, then you

will develop the trust needed to build the business here and keep it going forever. Switch your thinking from getting an order to getting reorders. When you do that, you understand why it is so important to secure trust in the relationship.

In the next chapter, we will look at communication.

2—Communication

P robably, you will be relying on your Japanese counterparty
to speak with you in English. Sadly, the education system
here is not pumping out fluent English speakers, and you
may be assuming the listener is understanding a lot more than
they are.

For a reality check, the next time you are flying on one of
the Japanese international airlines, have a careful listen to the
cabin crew when they switch to English. Often, these are young
women who are recent graduates. Listening to them, you can hear
that Japan still has a long way to go to catch up with the rest of
Asia when it comes to mastering English.

This has an impact when doing business here. Because Japan
looks like such a technologically advanced nation, our expectations
for English skills are automatically high. And due to the politeness
of the culture, people won't tell you they couldn't understand. That
would imply that you were not clear enough or you spoke too quickly.

To avoid offending you, they will not show that they are not
understanding. They will say nothing. You imagine all is fine and,
in fact, you probably even speed up your speech a little.

Therefore it is always good practice to check for understanding.
Go back and summarise what you said and see if they were following it. Speak more slowly. You need to slow it right down and
eliminate idioms, which are mostly impenetrable for Japanese
speakers of English.

I only discovered how much we use idioms when I was
interpreting for Australian exporters trying to crack the Japanese
market. Well, maybe it is an Australian thing, but we have so
many idioms and they are very hard for non-native speakers to
understand. There are national differences when it comes to idioms as well. I found we Aussies have developed quite a few that
even other native speakers have no clue about. So, to aid better
communication, remove idioms, sporting references, and slang
from your conversation.

For important meetings, always bring your own interpreter. They will be working for you and can help you to understand what is being said, what is not being said, and about how the members of the buying team are reacting. When the other side provides the interpreter, all they will tell you is what they want you to know.

Importantly, you need to brief your interpreter very well to get the most value. While interpreters may be really good at languages, they are usually not business people. They may be Japanese—and they may speak great English—but they have probably not done a lot of business in your line of work. So, they need your help. Don't skimp on the briefing for them or leave it until you are in the taxi on the way to the meeting.

In the West, we are getting more and more informal in business. Japan, however, is still a very formal country. Don't imagine that what works for you at home will work here.

Always bring business cards, and make sure you have more than you think you will need. You do not want to run out. The business card is a valuable tool for Japanese people to keep track of who they meet and to understand your rank inside the company. If you have some knowledge of kanji, always check the Japanese side of the counterparty's business card, because the English title and the Japanese title may be different.

Don't put their card in your shirt pocket or leave it lying around. Make sure you look at it carefully. If you don't have a business card holder, then stick it in your wallet so you are showing the person that they are important to you.

Always hand your cards over one by one. Emphasise the personal touch. I remember once when I was in a business meeting in a foreign country. The person I was meeting did have a business card, but upon entering the room they casually flicked it across the table to me. After living in Japan for such a long time, I almost had a conniption because of the shock. Never forget: a person's business card is an extension of their "face" and "honour".

When speaking Japanese, either go all the way in or leave it at a light level. The Japanese side won't be expecting you to have any

Japanese skills. If you know some phrases, this might be considered cute; but nobody takes it seriously.

Some buyers prefer that you don't know much Japanese, because they feel more in control. They can speak freely amongst themselves. Fluent speakers of Japanese can be seen as more of a problem, because it means you have peeled away a lot of their protective layers. If you know the language, then you know the culture—so they can't easily snow you. You know about how things work, so they know they can't tell you a bunch of crap and get away with it.

Save the humour for after-work drinks. Japanese meetings can be very formal and a bit heavy, so there is the temptation to lighten up the meeting with humour—the idea being that, if we use humour, we will somehow be able to become more friendly and closer to one another.

My Australian clients, coming from such a laid-back country, found the rigid formality of meetings in Japan very uncomfortable. They felt out of their depth and in very alien territory. They immediately tried to use humour to break down the formality and get the atmosphere more relaxed and closer to something they were more used to. Remember: the Japanese side has no issue with formality. Only you are having an issue with it. You are in Japan, and that is how they do things. So, be flexible and go with it.

Business is a serious affair in Japan. You don't have to lighten up the atmosphere, and you won't become instant buddies just because you are cracking some impenetrable jokes and engaging in light banter. Leave all that for dinner and drinks at night with the clients. This is when you will find the Japanese side really lightening up, in stark contrast to the atmosphere during the day.

In the next chapter, we will look at distribution.

3—Distribution

P roper due diligence is a must when you approach the Japanese market. Sounds pretty obvious. However, that doesn't prevent business people from doing the craziest things. Don't rely on getting into business with the Japanese businessperson sitting next to you on a plane. Amazingly, this random selection process happens more often than you might imagine.

Instead, use the trade promotion organisations from your home country and JETRO, the Japan External Trade Organization, to access possible business partners. These are all neutral parties, with good contacts in Japan, and they will either already know who to approach or can help you create a target list.

You might be thinking, "what would a bunch of bureaucrats know?" Well, guess who they have working for them: a large number of Japanese industry specialists. These people have been doing their jobs for years, and have built up terrific databases and personal connections.

There are also private consultancies that can help, and you should make use of them. Yes, you have to pay fees, but this is the third-largest economy in the world we are talking about here, with an impenetrable language you cannot speak or read and business customs which are highly unique. Japan is a long-term play, so approach it that way and get the best match of local partner from the start. It is much harder to unwind a bad choice later. Spend the money and time at the start and get the right business partner in Japan.

I have one strong piece of advice, having seen this go the wrong way in the past. That guy you met on the plane works for a huge corporate, and you have dollar signs in your eyes. You imagine that you are going to plaster the Japanese market with your products through this awesome new connection. "If we have Megacompany as our distributor, we are going to be huge in Japan".

Great. But never, ever get into an exclusive arrangement, unless there are targets and milestones in that agreement which will let you out if the Japanese partner doesn't perform. Some big companies will go for exclusive distribution arrangements, because they want to freeze you out of the market, since you may disrupt their current distribution alliances.

Also, you don't have to go after the largest partners. Japan is a very big economy, and there are provincial cities which are very large economies in their own right. So, you can find many players outside of Tokyo who are large enough to bring your products into Japan. Sometimes, this makes more sense because your production capacity may not be able to handle the needs of the whole country. You can also start in one local area and then add another, and another. This slow build allows you to gain valuable experience in the market without having to blow up your funding stash to develop the new business.

If you have the capacity to start your own distribution in Japan, look at that possibility carefully. You will have much more control over the pricing, positioning in the market, branding, etc. Over the past twenty years, we have seen many big retail brands go it alone without their local partners. The control element has been driving that desire to change the arrangements.

One good thing here is that the infrastructure is incredible. Internal shipping really benefits from the highways, bridges, amazing tunnels through mountains, ports, etc. The rail system is well developed and there are many local airports. Domestic transportation costs, however, can be expensive. I remember that, from Yokohama, it was cheaper to ship a container to Hamburg, Germany, than to Niigata, just a few hundred kilometres away on the coast of the Sea of Japan. If you have deep pockets, you might look at that direct distribution approach yourself. If not, then you have little choice but to use a local distributor.

The staff working for your distributor will have a huge range of products to sell apart from yours. So, you need to think about how you can support them as they come to understand your product. You need them to like you, because these personal relationships make the difference between them introducing a buyer to your product or your competitor's product.

If you can do it, accompany the local distributor on visits to the top 20% of their buyers who represent 80% of the sales. Go to them and say "thank you for buying our product". Often, the local distributor won't support that idea, because they worry you are trying to cut them out and go direct. You have to emphasise that you want to support them and grow the business. Those on the receiving end of the visit will be touched, because nobody visits them to say thank you. Japan doesn't appear to be an emotional country, but it is surprisingly emotional in business, and little things like this count for a lot here.

You should also visit Japan regularly to keep the personal connections alive. Don't think that you can put everything on automatic pilot and forget about it, leaving everything up to the local distributor. Come here often and work closely with your distributor—and their salesforce, in particular.

In the next chapter we will look at negotiations.

4—Negotiations

We sit across the table from the Japanese side and assume they are all united and on the same page. That may not be the case. Often, the people in the meeting are representing the various vested interests that will be impacted by the deal. Some of these people won't want the deal to proceed, because it changes the current arrangements. They don't want that to happen. The *ringi seido* system, in which people apply their seal to a document to signify they have read and approved it, means that decision-making is much more dispersed in Japan compared with Western countries.

Don't rely on the client's side to provide the interpreter for you. Bring your own. They will be able to give you valuable feedback on how they feel the other side is thinking about your proposal, what dynamics are driving the group, what the body language is saying, etc. To successfully gather this information, you need to brief the interpreter on what you want. Because they are rarely business people themselves, they won't necessarily know what to look for.

Don't imagine that the good English speaker on the buyer side is your friend, or that they have much power inside the buying team. They usually won't have much impact on the final decision, but we tend to gravitate toward them because we can easily communicate with them. They work for the buyer. Their careers are with the buyer. Never forget that when you are getting nice and chummy.

Don't go in at your best price in an attempt to be competitive. The Japanese side will see that as a starting point from which they will try to negotiate the price down further. Come in with a good price and always have a trade-off between price and other things, such as warranties, volumes, and timing of payment.

Determine your BATNA—your Best Alternative to a Negotiated Agreement or your walk-away position—in advance. Don't imagine that, by going super low in the pricing, you will be able to walk the price back up. It won't happen very easily. That low number will be the number—and it won't rise. No matter how much you try to condition the buying side to understand that this low price is a one-off—a special, once-only offer—they will ignore all that and just concentrate on the low-ball number you have agreed to. They will keep that number as the price and then try and drive you down from there.

Don't tell the other side your travel plans—especially not when you will be leaving. Time is a negotiating tactic, and they have plenty of time on their side. Japanese buyers are risk averse, and they feel no pressure. They know you are under pressure to get a deal cut or you go home empty handed, which won't be greeted enthusiastically back at head office. They know all of that, so they will try to use time pressure to cut a deal that favours them.

If they ask, tell them it is open ended, that there is no cut-off point. Don't book a ticket without the opportunity to change it. You will need as much flexibility as possible to get yourself into a good position in the deal.

Also, getting a deal on a single trip to Japan is unlikely. You may need to make a number of trips to build the relationship and cement the deal. Keep coming back, because this shows your commitment and reliability.

If you have to walk away, then do so. There are many players here in Japan, and they are not all concentrated in Tokyo. You will find sizeable companies in Japan's 47 prefectures, and there will be good business to be done with a big player in a local market. You can build a business over time—prefecture by prefecture—and not even have to worry about doing a deal in Tokyo.

In the next chapter, we will look at contracts.

5—Contracts

Contracts in Japan are not worth the paper they are written on. We are very legalistic in the West, and contracts define how business is done. In Japan, business is a series of interlocking relationships. The buyer and seller are looking to have a long-term relationship based on trust and mutual benefit. If the business situation of the buyer changes, then they expect the supply arrangements to follow suit. The fact that the contract specifies something else is considered irrelevant.

If the situation has changed, then the contract arrangements have to change. In the West, if the situation changes, too bad—the contract is what was agreed and that is that. If you don't like it, then see you in court. In Japan, litigation is rarely used to sort out contractual disagreements. Of course, when the contract amounts are huge, then yes, everyone resorts to the courts. Even then, the courts encourage companies to come to an agreement that doesn't need to be ruled on. Small and medium-sized companies are often operating in the no-contract world of trust. We are one of them.

Now, if you are a smaller company dealing with a big company and your situation changes, the bigger company will expect you to wear it. If their situation changes, then they expect you to be flexible. If you want to continue with them as your client, you are expected to take the long-term view and suck it up.

In my company's case, we rarely do contracts for the supply of our training services. It is very old style here. We agree and strike a "gentleman's agreement" to work together. I recall an amazing contract, though, that we had with a multi-national company. It was a very long and complex document with lots of penalties if we didn't follow their determinations. In one of the clauses, I noted that it said that, by signing this contract, we agreed to forgo the ability to settle any disputes in a court of law. Wow!

I was wondering to myself, "How could that clause be in there?" What sort of lawyer would write such a clause? If I don't pay them, how will they get their money if there is no court procedure involved?

If we did have a dispute, are they going to send a bunch of thugs around to my place with baseball bats? This is the crazy world of Western litigation.

We have never used contracts with Japanese companies here. Yet, in 10 years of my being in the company, we have not a single case in which we didn't get paid. There have been cases, though, where we have been forced to be flexible. The situation for the buyer changed and we had to accept the change, which actually went against us financially. If we wanted the relationship to continue, then there were no choices available but to do just that.

This is how it works. The big guys get what they want, and the little guys put up with it. Is that fair? No. Is it going to change anytime soon? No. So, when dealing with Japanese companies, we have to see the big picture, the long term.

Are there evil, unscrupulous, rip-off businesspeople here? Of course—but perhaps not as many as in other places. You have to be aware, but you shouldn't be putting all your faith in the piece of paper. Yes, you might get paid according to the contract, but that will probably be the last one with that company. You have to make a decision about how long you want to play in Japan. If in it for the long haul, then get ready to be flexible. Get ready to be shoved around unfairly sometimes, too.

These are general comments. The size of the deal will influence what happens in a given situation. The strategy of the seller in the market will also influence what happens. Generally speaking, though, don't expect contracts to protect you if you are the supplicant. When push comes to shove, you will get shoved. Harden up.

In the next chapter, we will look at speed.

6—Speed

S peed is very important in business. That's especially true in Japan—except when it comes to making decisions. This is when things really bog down, and it can drive you nuts. The various parties who may be impacted by the decision have to be consulted. There has to be agreement internally before anything can happen. Getting all that to occur, normally takes up a lot of time.

There is also the reluctance to take any risk, which starts slowing things down. Nobody wants to catch flack if things go wrong. The best way to avoid that? Don't do anything. From a Japanese viewpoint, it is better to hasten slowly. Nobody gets rewarded for making a quick decision in this country, but plenty of people will suffer if things go wrong.

However, once the decision is made, then everyone expects things to roll out promptly. There are people down the food chain who want to know the situation status, how much progress has been made, if the milestones are going to be met, if the project will stay on budget, if there are any problems, if everything is on track, etc. They will be coming to you for those answers, and they expect to be told straight away.

They have calmly forgotten that they took an age to make a decision. That is all now well back in the mists of time. They are fully concentrated on making sure everything runs to plan and that there will be no issues which may make them look bad. They want confirmations, tonnes of information, and as much data as they can get. This is all behaviour driven by supreme risk reduction.

We in the West tend to operate in the opposite manner. We are very quick to make a decision, but we are very casual in our execution speed. Japan, especially, moves quickly. The pace of life here is fast. In my hometown of Brisbane, conversely, the pace is quite a bit slower. I recall a seminar I attended many years ago in Australia, at which the speaker was relating his experience with Japanese buyers. He was in the granite rock export business. Huge slabs of granite would be shipped off to Japan for more high-precision cutting.

He noted that he often received faxes from Japan which were stamped URGENT. Here were these Japanese buyers writing to him in English, and stamping URGENT on the documents, using a stamp written in English. He wryly noted that he had grown up in Australia, in an English-speaking environment, and had been in business for a number of years, yet he didn't possess any stamp with the word URGENT on it. Dealing with Japanese buyers who have quite a different notion of urgency can get you tied up in knots pretty quickly.

The solution is to be quick with the turnaround. So, try to reply immediately. This gives the impression of urgency and a strong sense of support to the buyer side. You come across as someone they can trust, someone who understands their need for feedback so they can, in turn, inform others.

Dealing with Japan from Brisbane was easy, because there was just a one-hour time difference. Europe and the US are much more difficult—especially the US. Nevertheless, make a point to rapidly reply to enquiries if you want to establish a reputation for reliability. Reduce the friction of dealing with you by reducing the time it takes to get answers or action.

In the next chapter, we will look at getting paid.

7—Getting Paid

Nothing happens in commerce without a sale being made. Great to know that, but what about being paid for the sale? Now, in some countries, this can be an issue. We find ourselves swimming with sharks who are transactional in their thinking and have no hesitation in ripping us off. Fortunately, Japan usually isn't in that category.

We have rule of law in Japan, plus a very healthy moral code. Japanese people abide by the law—they line up nicely for trains and buses, there is hardly any road rage, they consider others, and they don't take other people's belongings. You are not going to get your bag or phone stolen by some expert Japanese gang who has the lift sequence down pat.

You see those videos from other countries in which gangs work as a team. One person distracts you, another lifts the bag off your shoulder, and another receives the bag and makes off with it. All this while yet another scouts for the constabulary. This doesn't happen often here in Japan, if at all.

If you drop your wallet, chances are the wallet—along with all cash and credit cards that were inside—will be returned intact to a police box. I have had that experience. Or, you might find it sitting on a ledge in a prominent position so you can easily find it when you go looking after discovering it is missing. I once dropped a keyholder near my house and, sure enough, even a few days later, it was still sitting there for me to find.

Now, this is not a nation of 126 million saints. Yes, there are yakuza, petty criminals, housebreakers, con men, and other assorted scoundrels operating here. However, Japan is a lot better than most other places, and this spills over into how business is conducted. We have been operating our business for 10 years and have never had a bad debt. You will get paid in Japan, unless you are particularly unlucky.

The issue here isn't so much *if* you will get paid, but rather *when* you will get paid. Cash flow is always of strong interest to small and medium-sized companies, and the timing can be crucial at different circumstances. If sales haven't been all that great, and the expenses are as high as ever, not getting the payment when you expect it can put pressure on your cash flow. Run out of cash, and you are out of business pretty promptly. Reputation for reliability in business is very important here. Lose that, and people won't work with you ever again. You are toast.

Counter-intuitively, the worst payers are the biggest players. The giant multi-nationals have clever chief financial officers who have worked out that they can screw the small guys and make them wait for 60 days or more before having to pay them. This is a case of might against right, and you have to take it if you want to do business with them. We don't like it, but we take it.

Major Japanese corporates pay you in 30 days, for the most part. Japanese domestic companies sometimes have tricky conditions, though. If your invoice isn't received by the 12th or the 15th of the month, then it won't get paid until the end of the next month. Or, they will not accept an invoice until the goods or services have been received—no payment in advance is possible. Or, they won't accept the electronic version, so you have to mail them a paper copy. Or, they find a minor mistake in the way you have captured the company name—or the name of the person on the invoice is wrong—and the accounting department won't accept the invoice. You must re-issue it, and the whole payment process starts from that date. Very picky at times, but all of this adds up to delays around when you get the money.

So, when starting a business relationship with a buyer, you have to ask the key questions:

- By which day of the month must the invoice be received?
- Will you accept an electronic invoice?
- How long are your payment terms?
- Do you have any protocols about advance versus subsequent payment?

You need to know these things for your own cash-flow planning. The good news is that you *will* get paid in Japan. The bad news is you may not get paid as quickly as you require.

In the next chapter, we will look at recruiting staff.

8—Recruiting Staff

Demographics are accentuating the talent shortage in Japan. The supply of young people has halved over the past 20 years and is on track to halve again between now and 2060. The number of young Japanese studying overseas peaked before the 2008 Lehman Shock, topping out at a bit over 80,000 per year. After the financial crisis, that number dropped to the low 50,000s. Today, it has crawled back up to about 60,000.

The flavour of their overseas experience has also changed. Many more are going for short stays, so their English doesn't become as good and their cultural immersion is not as deep. This is a function of cost, and also of greater concern about personal safety in a world where terrorists roam major cities, killing innocents without warning.

This trend of going abroad less frequently and for shorter periods is ironic, because the minds of the corporate titans in Japan are now more focused globally. Their companies need young Japanese staff who can handle the world beyond the seas surrounding Japan. They know that they have to acquire businesses and expand in markets offshore to survive the shrinking consumer base resulting from population decline.

Matrix organisations have Japanese staff here who lead foreign staff scattered around the world. The opposite is also true. Japanese staff here are reporting to foreign bosses located overseas. The old days of the simple model, in which the Japanese expat disappears for five years to be forgotten, are gone.

The English proficiency being produced by Japan's educational system is underwhelming. The system is failing young people. Instead of helping them gain a facility for English, it is making sure they hate having to learn it.

We live in a world where English capability is needed more than ever, and it is happening at the precise point when young people are opting to stay in Japan. It is hard to argue with their logic—the food is seriously excellent, there are no guns, no terrorists, no major drug problems, and everything is pretty comfortable. Why put yourself in the position of needing to deal with foreigners with your poor English? Better to stay here and relax.

The recruiting companies are having a field day, charging commissions of 35% or more to locate new staff. If you are a mega corporation, then this is probably a fleabite. If you are a small or medium-sized operation, it looms large. For example, a position with an annual salary of $100,000 will cost you $35,000 to place. That number will get your attention every time. There are job boards, and there are recruiter–job board combinations, but none of this is cheap.

In Japan, young people are encouraged by their families to join very large corporates. This seems a safe and stable selection process. Getting them to quit their current job to come and work for us is difficult. They will run into opposition from their parents—and even from their spouse's parents—when trying to make such a move. Foreign corporates might be angels, but everyone prefers the devil they know.

So, to encourage people to join, we must accentuate our flexibility. Not requiring people to work overtime or stay until 11:00 p.m. is well regarded. We can be more flexible than the big Japanese corporations.

Usually, there will be a base salary and a bonus arrangement. In the West, the bonuses are based on performance. In Japan, the bonuses are paid in summer and winter, and are more a delayed salary payment than a true bonus.

Western companies can pay for performance though, and this is a good differentiator. In Japanese companies, everyone gets paid the same and moves up through the ranks together, regardless of performance. It revolves around when you entered the company, how old you are, what rank you hold, etc. Everyone moves up together in lockstep. So, to get people to come aboard, you need to pay them more to compensate for the risk of joining you. And English speakers come at an additional premium.

One group which may become more important is the *dai ni shin sotsu* (second new graduates). These are young people in their mid-to-late twenties who have taken their first job after graduation but would like to change companies quickly—something traditionally uncommon in Japan.

The percentage of graduates who fall into this group is in the low thirties at the moment, but has reached the mid-forties in the past. According to the global recruiting company Disco, 43% of first-year recruits are already looking at the possibility of changing jobs. You spend one or two years training them, and then they may leave for greener pastures. That will hurt. Those pastures are no better than yours, but young people don't have the perspective that comes with experience to know that. Right or wrong, it doesn't matter because they are possibly going to leave anyway.

The worst scenario involves those who have spent about four or five years with the company, have been trained by you, and then walk out the door. They are on average 26 or 27 years old, and are difficult and expensive to replace. So, we really need to work hard at keeping the new recruits inside the company. This is the skill of the leader, and if they don't have the skills then you will see your good people walk out the door.

In the next chapter, we will look at staff engagement.

9—Staff Engagement

According to our global research, there are three critical issues that determine the level of engagement and one key trigger point to getting engagement. This global research was duplicated here in Japan and showed the same trends. The relationship between the staff member and their supervisor or boss is an obvious make-or-break point for getting high levels of engagement. What is your relationship with the team?

Often, we are promoted on the basis of our ability and our smarts. Then we find that we are leading people who are not like us. We think that being smart is enough, but, actually, when it comes to leading and engaging the team, our emotional quotient—or EQ—is much more important than our IQ. When we start a new business, there is so much pressure and we are so time poor that we often forget about the impact we have on the people around us. We forget to thank them, to encourage them, to coach them.

As the old saying goes, we don't leave companies, we leave bosses. Now, in many cases, they don't actually leave. They stay put, but they are not fully engaged. They are there to collect their pay and do the minimum possible to stay out of trouble. So, making staff feel valued and helping them grow is the first critical issue.

The second critical issue is the level of trust—on the part of the troops—with the direction in which senior management is taking the company. The degree to which the people at the bottom believe the people at the top know what they are doing, has a strong influence on engagement. This sounds simple, but often the internal communication mechanisms from those at the top to those at the bottom are not working well.

When people don't know the WHY, it is hard for them to sign on for the journey. We may think we have fully explained the vision and mission, and that the troops get it. This is rarely the case. We have to keep hammering those key messages over and over again, because people do not get it from one telling. Middle Management should be reinforcing the key messages from the top, but often they are not.

Instead, they are soaking up all the information from above but are not passing it on. The people at the bottom do not have a clear idea of the rationale for decisions or changes in direction, because no one has sufficiently explained it to them.

The third critical issue revealed by the survey of engagement was pride in the company. When you work for a big-name brand, or a big powerful company, it is easier to feel pride in what you are doing. But for small and medium-sized enterprises, we have to work hard to create that pride.

Battles between internal silos is a factor of modern corporate divisional life. This is directing energy and focus away from the rivals out there in the market. The silo leaders complain about other parts of the organisation, and this doesn't help to build a strong sense of engagement within the organisation. This is a weakness in the leadership, because they don't know how to engage the team from a holistic point of view.

I had a case in which a client's key opponent in the market had been disorganised and wasn't much of a rival. But they were changing, they were improving, they were on the way to becoming a strong rival. This is a perfect launch pad from which to build engagement. You can unite the team against those rivals and galvanise people's energy and attention. Have the offsite meetings, the dinners, the after-work drinks—anything that will help people on the inside bond against the enemy on the outside.

The key trigger point to engagement is feeling valued. Everyone is working away in their role, but do they understand where they fit into the big picture? Where their little job makes a difference? Where they make a difference? For a lot of admin jobs, it is hard to feel as if anything you are doing means anything.

We must have those conversations where we reassure everyone that what they are doing is important, and that they are important. One of the issues is that we forget to tell them, because we think either they already know or they don't need to know. They should be able to work it out for themselves, we think. Well, they can't, and they need to have their importance and value to the organisation constantly reinforced through the communication skills of the leader.

In a time-poor world, we can find ourselves moving from one meeting to another and shooting out orders like a machine gun in the interval. This is not going to engage anyone. And where is the "feeling valued" part? You might think you are doing this now—and doing it sufficiently—but you may be fooling yourself.

If you are brave enough, you can do a quick self-audit and confirm how much of your time, during a typical week, is actually spent communicating to the troops that they are valued in this organisation. I don't mean how much time you spent barking out orders at them—I mean praising them. Get the smelling salts ready.

In the next chapter, we will look at networks.

10—Networks

In business, the ability to develop a strong network is critical. There is nothing better than getting to know buyers through these networks and establishing a personal connection. Japan is the premier nation on the planet for networks. When I first came here in the spring of 1979, I was taken to a *ryokan* (a traditional Japanese inn) which had a hot spring bath. That evening, we could hear this raucous party going on in one of the restaurants next door. It turned out to be the annual reunion for graduates of the local elementary school. I was thinking, "I hadn't seen anyone from my elementary school in decades, and had lost touch with them completely." Not here in Japan. Here, they are much better organised. The middle schools, high schools, and universities are excellent at getting everyone together for reunions. They are probably unsurpassed in this skill anywhere in the world.

There are also many formal business organisations. Keidanren (the Japan Business Federation) and Keizai Doyukai (the Japan Association of Corporate Executives) are big, powerful bodies. However, you won't even get a look into joining those unless you are a major company. Keieisha Kyokai (the Employers' Association) may be a better possibility, as we have been able to join it. There is also the Tokyo Chamber of Commerce, which will be easy to join.

Rotary clubs in Japan are also very business oriented, in the sense that Japanese businesspeople comprise the membership. There are lots of clubs, and you can visit others in addition to the one of which you are member—so you are not restricted to just the one group. My own club, the Tokyo Rotary Club, has 330 members and is full of big-hitters.

There are also a number of private business clubs such as Tokyo American Club and The Tokyo Club. I am a member of both. Others include The Kojun Club, The Kobe Club, the International House of Japan, Roppongi Hills Club, Ark Hills Club, the Tokyo Lawn Tennis Club, the Yokohama Country & Athletic Club, For Empowering Women Japan (FEW), and the College Women's Association of

Japan (CWAJ). Some can be very hard to get into, but those groups will have lots of influential members who you want to meet.

There are also many, many friendship associations such as the Japan-British Society, the Japanisch-Deutsche Gesellschaft, the Australia Society and the Tokyo Canadian Club. These tend not to be business oriented, but you can still meet business people socially.

If you have children here in Japan and are sending them to international schools, then the PTA is a great place to meet people. You will find that the captains of industry are sending their children to these same schools, and you can meet them through that avenue. I have been the president of the Parent Faculty Advisory Board at my son's school and have met many leading business people through that connection.

Then there are the various chambers of commerce. In the case of my company, we are—or have been—a member of the American Chamber of Commerce in Japan, the British Chamber of Commerce in Japan, the French Chamber of Commerce and Industry in Japan, the German Chamber of Commerce and Industry in Japan, the Australian and New Zealand Chamber of Commerce in Japan (of which I am Emeritus President), and the Italian Chamber of Commerce in Japan. And there are many more. All of these chambers are full of people who you would want to meet to expand your network here in Tokyo.

Every major country has its own chamber, and, like us, you can join multiple ones. These groups hold regular meetings and events—especially the American chamber—so there is no shortage of things to attend. By way of example, the American chamber hosts at least two or three events every week, with speakers talking on different topics of interest. Actually, forget the topic. If you want to meet people, then pick a popular subject regardless of your personal interest and go. You will find 150 business people in the room ready to meet you.

There are also *benkyokai* (study groups). I belong to the High-Tech Study Group, the CEO Insights group, the Tokyo Entrepreneur group and the Foreign Corporate Communications (FCC) group.

There are many, many more clubs that I don't belong to, like the infamous Beef and Burgundy Club (The B&B), the Carbine Club, the Good Grub Club, the Wine and Food Society, Brits at Lunch, and the Foreign Correspondents' Club of Japan (FCCJ). And there are probably many others I have never heard of. These are great opportunities to build your connections and networks of people across a broad spectrum of industries and sectors. They usually meet regularly, have guest speakers, and allow you to mix with other leaders in town.

In the next chapter, we will look at customer service.

11—Customer Service

Japan is probably the leading country for customer service. These are seriously picky, picky local consumers here. If you are dealing with consumers in Japan, then you had better have your quality act together. Poor quality will not be tolerated. The expectations of Japanese consumers are extremely high, and they will complain vigorously if those standards are not being met.

It is often hard to understand. I grew up in Queensland, Australia, which is famous as a production centre for tropical fruit, such as mangoes. I planted and grew a mango tree in my backyard in Brisbane, and it produced beautiful fruit. What you would pay for an entire box of mangoes in Queensland is what you will pay for one Miyazaki mango in Japan. But that Miyazaki mango will be perfect. Absolutely perfect. No blemishes, no marks, perfect symmetry, and the taste will be sublime. This is high praise coming from a proud native Queenslander, I can assure you.

Now, in Japan, people will pay for quality—and this is the difference. In the rest of the world, people are more concerned with volume. In Australia, they would rather have the box at that price point than the single perfect mango. So, our concepts about what constitutes quality are fundamentally different.

Remember that most urban Japanese, who live in big cities such as Tokyo, rent or own a very small apartment. They actually can't acquire lots of stuff, because there is simply no place to put it. So, you want to have the best of what you can afford, given the space limitations. And, because there are few parks or sporting facilities, residents of these cities have selected two major leisure activities: eating and shopping. The locals are well prepared to spend money on both. As a result, they are quality conscious and demanding. This quality expectation transfers to service provision as well. Service in hotels and restaurants must be conducted at a high level.

If you are in the B2B area, then there are so many layers of distribution, and the relationship between each becomes very important.

Each layer alone doesn't hold a lot of stock, so the replenishment part must be working well. Everything is "just in time," like the Toyota system of car production. If you delay delivery, then you are disrupting the whole system and everyone will complain vigorously up the food chain, until it gets to you. You don't want that. The mutual dependencies here work because everyone understands the importance of quality and timeliness.

The level of quality provision is so high that the buyer expects to receive more than they are paying for. They expect to get advice, very fast follow-up, and that you are available all the time to answer their questions. Speed of reply to emails and phone calls becomes more important.

In many countries, if you send an email and you don't get an answer until the next day—or the one after—most people are okay with that. In Japan, if someone sends an email to me in the morning and there is no quick reply, they are soon ringing me or emailing me again to find out the information. This is, again, an example of that interconnectivity phenomenon. Everyone has promised something to someone else along the food chain. They have to keep reporting that everything is on track. In this regard, Japanese buyers have an insatiable appetite for information and reporting.

Ironically, when they make a decision, they take an age to get there. Things drag out interminably, nothing seems to be happening, time passes, and we grow old. Then, suddenly, the decision is reached and all hell breaks loose. Now everyone wants everything yesterday, and they expect you to provide that level of service. We tend to be rather zen—"less is more"—in the West, whereas Japan is often more baroque, "more is better".

Japanese people like to keep in touch to a degree we can't imagine. For example, we get gifts for *Oseibo* at the end of the year, gifts for *Ochugen* during the middle of the year. They send me Christmas cards, New Year's cards, and start of summer cards. They do these things during these traditional gift-giving periods to keep in touch and to remind you that they are there to serve you. I am expected to be doing the same to my buyers.

People will drop in unannounced, without an appointment. One of my staff will come to me and say, "So and so is here to see you". I think to myself, "Did I forget an appointment?" So, I check my diary and find that there is no appointment. They are just dropping by to say hello and to remind me that they are here to serve me. My buyers expect this from me as well. This is not how we do business in the West, so there is quite a different expectation here about what it means to have a business relationship. Japan sees Western business as "dry". They prefer "wet". This is the contrast between efficiency and empathy in business. Here, EQ is higher up the scale of importance than IQ.

This is all very time-demanding in a time-poor world. But that is the expectation, and you have to understand the point. You cannot over-communicate with Japanese companies. Their tolerance for over-communication is very much higher than ours.

In the next chapter, we will look at the art of networking in Japan.

12—Networking

There are two varieties of networks here for me: the Japanese-speaking ones and the English-speaking ones. With regards to the Japanese-speaking groups, there are a few things which are a bit different. Japanese people are raised not to talk to strangers. And guess what? They carry this over to networking events. At a typical Japanese event, if I know you and I meet someone else whom I know, I will introduce the two of you. I won't walk up to a complete stranger and start introducing myself.

At least that is what I would do if I followed how it is typically done here. But this limits how many people you can meet at an event. In our case, with my team, we bowl straight up to strangers at networking events and introduce ourselves. If you are going to create a contact with someone new, you have to make it happen. Be polite and be reasonable, but you have to break through the barriers.

I also recommend you do your best to connect the people you have met with people you already know. Japanese people are shy about breaking into groups who know each other and are busily chatting away. You can help this newfound friend of yours to enlarge their networking circle by bringing them into the group. They will definitely appreciate it. We should model some of the possibilities available through better networking efforts.

As a foreigner, the social rules are not as strict for me compared with my Japanese team members. Often, I am the battering ram, walking up to groups standing around in a circle and breaking in. I then introduce my staff member, and away we go. I just keep repeating this all evening, and we get to meet a lot of new people and some potential clients.

With English-speaking events, there are two varieties of potential contacts: those who are Japanese and those who are foreigners. The Japanese always get there early and go straight to the tables, where they sit scrolling on their phones, either uninterested or unable to meet anyone. I don't let that little detail stop me. I walk straight up to them on their right shoulder and introduce myself. "May I meet you? My name is Greg Story," I say as I extend my business card to them. They are usually a bit taken aback, because they thought they were safe from having to meet anyone new. But after the conversation starts, they warm up.

You might be thinking, "why the right shoulder?" Most people are right handed, and it is easier to reach into your coat pocket—or your bag for ladies—to locate your business card holder to do the card exchange.

If you go in pairs, basic Rule Number One is: Don't sit at the same table. How are you going to meet anyone new if you sit together? My rule is: Divide up the room. I will take this half; you take the other half. We will get back together at the end and exchange notes on whom we met at the event. This sounds simplistic, but so many times I meet people sitting together who are from the same company. Why would you do that?

I try to start with the people standing around at the beginning of the event. Then I move on to those sitting at other tables, leaving my own table until last. The organisers will be harassing people to sit down so that the food can be served. Ignore that command completely and keep meeting people now that they have sat down. You will have missed some at the start, when everyone arrived. Here is the chance to fix that. I walk around meeting everyone at the other tables and then, finally, make my way to my own. I will have a chance to engage with the people there over lunch. You usually only have a few minutes when you walk around working the tables, but you have about 30–40 minutes over lunch to engage with your tablemates.

The organisers sometimes provide a list of who has signed up to attend the event. This is very handy. If they haven't done that, it is always good practice to get there early and check the name badges—all beautifully lined up for you in alphabetical order. This allows you to put a face to the name of those people you have already met, and to identify some people you may want to meet. It is also good practice to ask the organisers to introduce you to people you want to get to know, or at least to point out who is who so that you can go and introduce yourself.

As a basic rule, I try to position myself right near the door, so that I can meet people as they come in. The people I know, I can greet with their name, because I was reminded by their name card at the front desk. This cuts down the usual embarrassment of forgetting the name while recalling the face.

I recommend you always have a couple of key questions ready. We want them to do most of the talking. This will help you determine if the person is a potential client. Japan is very good because everyone carries business cards with a wealth of information therein. You can tell the company name, the person's position within the company, and where the office is located. When we chat with them, we have to use some hooks that will flag their interest in what we do. The hook is the springboard to getting a business meeting.

Now, the person's title may tell you they are not a decision-maker, but don't miss the chance to ask if they can introduce you to the decision-maker. If they are clearly not a potential client, then be charming but move on. Don't get stuck there chatting away with just one person. When I decide to move on, I do this very politely, saying, "Thank you, I have enjoyed meeting you and I am going to take the opportunity to meet a few more people today."

I am there to find potential clients. This is not a social activity to chat with people over lunch. I do that, too, but that is not why I am at the event. I want to build my contact base and find buyers. That is the point of networking: to know and to be known. We should be bold, because we have what their company needs, and it is our duty to make sure they get it. The object is to find potential clients using your hooks and then arrange to have a follow-up meeting in their office, after the event. Don't try and discuss the details of business in a crowded, noisy, public space. Greet them at the event, find out if there is some way you can be of service to them, and then arrange a follow-up meeting.

In the next chapter, we will look at presenting.

13—Presenting

J apan has some particular ways of doing things. You've heard the expression, "When in Rome, do as the Romans do". That would be extremely bad advice when it comes to presenting your solution to buyers here. Japan is the country of zen, which holds simplicity at its centre. You would never know that, though, looking at typical business presentations. They are a real mess. There are slides with five different colours on offer, you will see four or five different fonts on the same slide, the text will be dense and the font small, making the content impenetrable. If there are four graphs, then they are all shown on the same slide.

When one of my team showed me the slide deck from a recent presentation he attended, I didn't know whether to laugh or cry. This event, hosted by the illustrious Tokyo Chamber of Commerce, was attended by about 150 hopefuls who were keen and eager to learn how to do presentations properly. The instructor was a Japanese business consultant, and his slides were terrible. There were too many details on each, too much text, too many diagrams cobbled together on one screen. He was using four different fonts on each slide. It was ugly and hard to follow. He was someone—supposedly an expert on presentations—showing the faithful how to do it. Sadly, the lack of knowledge here on how to present is legendary.

I was once asked to give a series of presentations for the Tokyo Metropolitan Government on how to start a business in Japan. They showed me what the previous speaker, a Japanese businesswoman, had been using. I just laughed to myself when I saw it. It was florid, drenched in too many colours with too much text set in sizes that were too small. It was a total disaster as far as a professional business presentation goes. The officials at the Tokyo Metropolitan Government obviously thought that this mess passed muster.

How could that be? I don't know, because this is the country of high aesthetics and zen simplicity. But if you ever take a careful look at a Japanese kimono, you will find an amazing array of colours.

Often, these colours don't seem to go together—at least not as far as Western concepts of colour-matching go. Maybe there is more of a kimono mind at play in these presentation designs rather than any zen sensibility?

Even smart people do the craziest things. One of my ex-staff now works for a robotics company founded by a mad professor type. The founder is very, very smart. I attended his presentation and, boy oh boy, where did the smarts go? The slideshow was the same thing as I mentioned earlier. Too many colours and too much information crammed onto one slide. It was totally dense, over-loaded with diagrams, details, and graphs. An audience cannot follow this, so stay away from this Japanese model and instead create professional presentations that are concise, precise, clear, and sparse.

It is also quite common in Japan for people to sit down when they present. You will find that a desk, chair, and low microphone stand have been prepared for you. Don't do this. Stand up so that you can position yourself to the left of the screen as viewed from the audience. We want them looking at our face first, then reading left to right across the screen. We know that our face is the most powerful tool there is when it comes to presentations, and we want to be in the best position to use it. Also, when we stand up, we get to use the full capacity of our body language to drive home the key points we want to make.

However, in Japan, standing above the audience implies your eminent superiority over all those who are sitting. You simply can't imply that with buyers, because they are God; there is nothing higher than them. So, you need to make an apology letting them know that you are going to stand up, but that this will make it easi-er for you to give the presentation. This applies to foreigners and to Japanese alike.

If they expect you to sit, the key is to stand up, but to apol-ogise first. Through the apology, you should get some unspoken permission not to sit when presenting. For foreigners, we are freed up from a lot of this culture's restrictive conventions, because we are seen as ignorant, not knowing any better. This apology idea, though, travels very well across audiences and nationalities. Even if you have Japanese team members doing the presentation in Japanese, get them to apologise and stand up when they present.

Japan is not big on eye contact. They don't have that view that you can't trust people who can't look you in the eye. In fact, staring at people is considered offensive and aggressive. That "no eye contact" idea is fine for conversation, but presenting is a different occasion. Certainly use eye contact with the members of the audience, but make it no longer than six seconds at a time. This is enough time to engage with the audience member without burning a hole in their retina.

If you are presenting to a buying group, do not just imagine that you can engage with the main person and do the deal. The way decisions are made here, all the key stakeholders will be assembled in the room. Consensus is important, and they are all there to help them arrive at a consensus decision on dealing with you. Because of the inherent risk aversion so pronounced here, few people will want to say "yes" to anything new, because that is by definition risky. So, the group is there to make sure the deal is safe, or to make sure it doesn't happen at all. You need to engage everyone.

Also, don't make the beginner's mistake of talking to the person with the best English. They are rarely the decision-maker. They are just a minion who is there only because they have good English. Engage with everyone, just as you should be doing in any presentation.

In the next chapter, we will look at face.

14—Face

I f you enjoy a good debate, well, Japan is not the place for you. In Western culture, debating is part of the education system. What is a debate? It is an argument in which one team tries to outsmart the other, one-up them, show that they are superior, more intelligent, and more persuasive. It is a smarty-pants culture. Our love of oratory goes right back to the ancient Greeks and continues today. We admire people who are articulate, witty, and clever, and we are amused when someone successfully one-ups the other party.

I was raised in Australia, home to a macho culture in which boys are constantly trying to one-up each other. We do this in sports—especially extreme sports, such as seeing who can jump off the highest riverbank. The classic Aussie male conversation goes, "Hold my beer and watch this," as they go off and do some crazy thing.

This culture of being bigger, better, bolder, and brassier than someone else is completely different to Japan. Here, debating will never be fully embraced, because it is basically an argument. This is a land of harmony, consensus, cohesion, and calm. No arguments. The Japanese have been living on top of each other in highly dense societies for thousands of years. They have learnt how to get on with one other and how to avoid arguments.

We know this, but in business we sometimes forget. We may be very strong in a meeting, driving our point home to the audience be they buyers, suppliers, or our staff. This strength, however, can be interpreted as bullying. They feel we are trying to put them down, that we are being arrogant toward them. Preserving face is very important—especially when it comes to dealing with mistakes. Japan is a country of perfectionists, so a mistake is a big deal and represents a loss of face. In the bad old days, Japanese bosses would have no qualms about balling out a miscreant in front of the whole office. Today, the HR department will soon be hearing about a power harassment charge against the boss. How we handle mistakes— including our own—becomes very, very important.

We have to remember that our buyers, suppliers, and staff are very concerned with their face. The worst thing you can do is criticise someone publicly. This is a big no, no. They see this as an attack and affront. You may be 100% correct, but bully for you. They don't want to lose face in public, to be one-upped, to be argued with. You might win the battle, but you will lose the war in Japan.

We always have to consider the other person's face. We had a case with a client—a multinational company whose team is all Japanese—who had a very strict and robust legal contract which we had to sign. It had all these very detailed provisions and various penalties. It also said that if they cancelled the training within a certain super-tight time frame, we could invoice them for the full amount of the training. Sure enough, that is exactly what happened. By signed agreement, I could have sent them an invoice and they would have been duty bound to pay it. I didn't send that invoice, because I knew this would cause a loss of face for the HR team with whom we were working.

Someone inside the company would ask why this invoice must be paid when no training was delivered. They would have to admit their error and lose face. By not pursuing the matter, I saved them face. This is where we have to think beyond the obvious and the short term to how we can have a great relationship with our client. Yes, we lost money in the short term, but we kept the lifetime value of the client. It is the same with my own staff. I am a driver personality style, which means I am a go, go, go person with no patience, who consistently wants everything yesterday. I can be very demanding, but I have to be careful not to allow this to result in a loss of face for my team. I am not perfect at it, by the way, but I am thinking like that all the time. I don't debate. We have discussions, we trade ideas, but we don't argue. Being persuasive yes, but not trying to win the argument. If I win, you lose. This is not the best way to approach Japan. Remember: I win, and you lose face—that is a bad idea for succeeding in business in Japan.

In the next chapter, we will look at getting change.

15—Getting Change

G etting change anywhere is a difficult process, but Japan is a special case. Often in business here, we, as a foreign entity, represent the change. We are the potential new supplier, and that means a change. They have been doing business with someone else and we want them to stop doing that, to do business with us instead.

There are many currents underpinning Japanese culture and its resistance to change. I have been training in traditional Japanese karate for 48 years, and part of that process is learning set sequences called *kata*. These are fixed moves that cannot be varied in any way. There is but one way to do the movement, and our job is to replicate that same movement as demonstrated by the *sensei* for thousands of repetitions, until we have perfected it. There is no possibility of doing it a different way. In other words, no change is possible.

This is a powerful metaphor for many things in Japan, where there is only one way of doing things and it cannot be varied. This is prime change-resistance in action. I find this at home, too. My wife is Japanese, and there are certain things which must be done a certain way. Being an Aussie, I am pretty flexible on trying to do things in a different way; but she brooks no variation. There is a certain way which specific things must be done. And that is that.

This is baked into the culture, and here you are trying to break into the market. By definition, you *are* change, and there is change-resistance already in the culture from the start. Anything that represents a change for a company has to get signed off by all the stakeholders. This is the famous *ringi seido* system, in which everyone applies their seal to the piece of paper to show they are in agreement.

There will more resistance to change to diminish possible risk, than enthusiasm for something better. Part of this issue is that no one wants to take responsibility if problems arise, so the safest path is to say "no". Hence, a change in suppliers is not easy here. Risk aversion means they have worked out who is the most reliable and consistent partner in their supplier relationship. The existing supplier is the low-risk option. They have a track record and have built credibility over a long period of time.

You, however, are shiny and new. Maybe you are reliable. Maybe you are not. Who knows? So, no change is a better path forward for people who don't want to be accountable. We must come up with ways to eliminate or mitigate the risk. In our case, as a training company, we tell clients we will only ask one question after the delivery of the training: Are you satisfied? If the answer is no, then there is no debate, no haggling. The training is free and there is no cost to the company apart from the time they have invested.

We do this because we have to make it easy for the line manager or the HR managers to give us a chance to become a new supplier of training services. What about your case? What can you do to take away the risk of doing business with you? Remember, we are dealing with individuals who are deeply ensconced in their comfort zone. They have reduced risk in all aspects of their life. They are seeking the maximum efficiency, at the lowest cost and the fastest speed.

I am the same. I get up at the same time, catch the same train to work, choose the same carriage because it will be the closest to the stairs or escalator at the other end. I eat in the same 20 restaurants within a half a kilometre of my office. This comfort-zone reality is a resister to change. It encourages us to keep doing the same things over and over. We are doing the same thing in business— choosing the fastest, cheapest, safest way of doing things. That refinement makes it hard to break in when you are the angel they don't know. The opportunity cost of continuing with the same supplier, the Devil they do know, and not gaining benefit from a new supplier, is not easily considered.

The individuals we are dealing with are worried about themselves and not getting into any trouble. So, the same things get done, the same way, with the same results. This is just fine with them. Underperformance won't get you fired here in Japan, but mistakes can. We are new, we are a comfort-zone expander, a pattern disruptor. Because of this, we meet heavy resistance.

To persuade the company that we are the better option—all risks considered—we have to be working on more than just our champion inside the company. There are so many people who can say no, so we need to make sure we are working on them, too. Our champion has to be primed to take the argument to the doubters and convince them to give us a try.

It is possible to effect change here, because we do get new clients. It just takes a long time and is difficult. It is not uncommon to create a new client from someone we met two, three, even four years ago. We have been in business for 107 years—56 of those in Japan—but potential new clients still want to test us with a small amount of training first. Japan needs patience and extended time frames, and you must deal with that if you want to overcome the culture's inherent resistance to change. You need to make HQ understand this if you want to be successful here.

In the next chapter, we will look at formality.

16—Formality

Formality is linked very closely to what is perceived as politeness. Those from European countries may feel more familiar with Japanese-style formality, but in countries such as the United States, Australia, and Canada, this level of formality is not the norm. In Japan, there is a sense of formality that is unanticipated by most foreigners.

The most formal meeting I have ever attended in Japan was when I met previous-Emperor Akihito in his palace. When every new Ambassador arrives in Japan, they go to the palace to present their credentials. The Ambassadors don't go to the palace on their own, they have an entourage of senior officials from the embassy with them. I was in that group.

For these visits, you first go to a special waiting room at Tokyo Station and are then taken to the palace by horse-drawn carriage, led by a mounted escort. There are numerous points of protocol to follow when greeting the Emperor. How you walk, stand, move, speak, and sit are all important. Formal beyond words is how I would describe the atmosphere.

The second-most formal meeting I have been to in Japan was with some fishmongers in Osaka. I was introducing then Australian Ambassador Dr Ashton Calvert to various importers dealing with Australia. This seafood business was a large one, and a big buyer of Australian produce.

They had the entire echelon of senior management turn out for the meeting. It was a very stiff affair, a complete ceremony in itself. The formality was quite breath-taking. I never expected that fishmongers could be that formal, but it was a very serious affair, because of the "above God" status of the visiting Ambassador. In their minds, they were being polite, and the way to do that was through formality.

There are levels of politeness here with the accompanying formality. Even simple things such as how you sit. I had an embarrassing experience when I was attending a senior Australian government official making the rounds of calls in Osaka. The governor of Osaka was unavailable that day for the meeting, so we met the vice-governor.

Picture this: The vice-governor is sitting ramrod straight in his chair, with a 15-centimetre gap between his spine and the back of the chair, Roman patrician-style—very formal and upright. My Aussie VIP visitor, by contrast, was sitting there with his legs kicked out in front of him, sprawling back in his chair, like he was on his couch at home watching the footy. The contrast in informality and formality was stunning. The formality/politeness construct comes straight into play here. Is lounging around in a formal meeting polite in a Japanese context? Was my VIP showing any respect for the vice-governor? I don't think so. After the meeting, I tried to breach the subject of required formality in Japan with my visitor in a subtle way; but I failed. The cognition gap was too wide to straddle.

Japan's politeness is linked to formality and thoughtfulness. Japanese people are very, very thoughtful. Australia, where I grew up, is so much more easy-going, informal, and casual, so sometimes it is hard to get your head around Japanese formality. The thoughtfulness thing is also surprising, too. What are you doing to be thoughtful in business with your clients? What can you do for them?

When you go into the meetings, be more formal than normal. It will be seen as polite. Australia is probably the casual capital of the universe. That is fine in Australia, but Japan is different.

All of this flies out the window, however, when you go out drinking together. It is extremely informal, but that is the correct environment for that activity and Japan doesn't mix it together. The problem with a lot of informal countries, such as my own, is that we tend to want to mix them together, to be informal when we should be trying to be formal.

If you say, "No, I want to do it my way, this is how we do it in my country, I am not going to be Japanese about this," then good luck with that approach. Let me know how that is working out for you! I wouldn't recommend it. I suggest you try to be seen as polite in a Japanese context, and that means being a lot more formal than would normally be the case in a business setting.

You will never be Japanese. Ever. You will just never be considered Japanese by the Japanese, no matter how long you live here. Trust me. But you will be considered polite from their point of view, their reference point. We have to be conscious of that and maybe up the formality levels a bit to fit in—at least during working hours. After work, we are all champions of informality; so we already have that part down pat.

In the next chapter, we will look at *nemawashi* (groundwork).

17—*Nemawashi* (Groundwork)

Nemawashi is a very important word in Japanese. It is made up of two words: *ne*, which means root, and *mawashi*, which means to wrap around. So, it literally means wrapping around the root, but a good translation associated with a decision or a meeting is "groundwork".

The Japanese have the amazing ability to move 15–20-metre-tall trees from one location to another. They dig down, cut the tap root, wrap up the root ball, get a big crane, put the whole tree on a huge truck, and transplant it to another place. Quite incredible. That *nemawashi* represents preparation before the tree gets moved.

The same things apply in business. We want a certain decision to be taken, so we prepare to influence the direction that decision will take. We might be dealing with a client or someone within our own company. Japan doesn't leave anything to chance. Prior to the meeting, you meet with the other people who are going to attend and try to get their agreement with what you will propose. In this way, the decision is taken before anyone gets in the room and nobody loses face. The meeting itself is just there to formally approve what has been informally decided beforehand.

In a Western context, we would make the decision in the room. Everyone would turn up expecting that there will be a discussion, some debate, and then a final decision will be reached during that meeting. In a Japanese context, the decision will already have made before the meeting; so, if you want to influence the decision, you have to start early. It is no good leaving it until the meeting itself, because that will be too late. The decision will have already been taken.

If dealing with a client company, you need to work with your internal champion to get the decision-makers to agree with what you want to happen. Usually, the decision you want is for the client to use your product or service. As an outsider, you won't be in the internal meeting, but you still must help your champion be persuasive with everyone when laying the groundwork or *nemawashi*. Give them the data, the evidence, the testimonials, the conditions—whatever it takes to make the case solid when they present it to the people who will be in the meeting. Don't wait too long to do this, because it takes time to get around to everyone and have those discussions before the meeting.

Are the other people in the meeting who want a different decision or outcome doing their own *nemawashi*? Yes, absolutely they are. This is why you have to prepare your champion to be effective in making the argument in your favour. They can get the meetings, but they need your help to be persuasive. The quality of the preparation has a big impact on the final result, of course. You need to get them to nominate who will be in the meeting and get an idea of what will encourage those people to be in agreement with the decision you want. Your champion should have a game plan for each person, and that should be put together with your help.

If you understand that *nemawashi* represents the idea of preparation, then be well prepared. As pointed out, don't leave this process to the last moment. You need to give yourself time to allow the *nemawashi* system to work in your favour. You also need to anticipate the arguments of the other side and head those arguments off at the pass. You are working through your champion, so the preparation becomes even more important. Does it mean you will always prevail? No. You will win some and you will lose some. But by laying the groundwork, you will place yourself in the best possible situation to get a win.

If you had no idea about this *nemawashi* requirement, then you can probably begin to understand why the decision you wanted went against you. From now on, become part of the Japanese decision-making process and exert influence from within.

In the next chapter, we will look at another key Japanese word: *omotenashi*.

18—*Omotenashi*

O*motenashi* is a difficult word to translate. It is quality service which both anticipates and exceeds the customer's expectations. Few Western countries have any concept of anticipating the buyer's needs, let alone doing so and then exceeding them. The Japanese consumer is really well treated, and they are very, very demanding. We might even think it is nuts, but what we think is actually not of any great interest to the buyer. They want high quality, and that is that.

This is especially true in the service sector, and this high level of service seeps into other sectors because the Japanese buyer is so exacting. Even in the B2B environment, the seller is trying to anticipate and exceed the buyer's expectations. Remember, everyone here grows up with these standards and ideas about service quality. The business buyer is that same demanding consumer who is shopping or eating out on the weekend. They are used to being treated very well by everyone in a service or product provision role.

So, what we may see as good service in our home countries is probably only the bare minimum—or even less—by comparison with what is on offer in Japan. It is hard to understand the expectations of the Japanese buyer when your point of reference is what you are used to back home. You grew up with poor, mediocre, or maybe even truly bad service, and that is what you accept as normal.

To be successful, we must switch gears in our thinking of what constitutes quality service. We have to really elevate our concept of what good service is—from a Japanese perspective—and what we can expect our local rivals will be trying to provide. Often, we are the new entrant trying to supplant the current provider. Why would a company want to accept a drop in service quality by switching their buying over to us? Well, they wouldn't, which is why we have to step up our game here in Japan.

Take our industry. Thinking about the likely buyers in that sector, and our product or service, what could we do that would constitute an *omotenashi* level of service? This is not a simple process, but we have to research the buyer, their needs and expectations, and really get a clear picture of what *omotenashi* means to them.

That whole idea is a very positive one, though, that transcends Japan. If you can provide the high levels of service required in Japan, and you can replicate that level of service in your home markets, you will do very, very well. Your home-market competitors won't be able to compete with you very easily anymore. So, the effort to match the required levels of service here—though very challenging—ultimately could give you a global advantage. If you can replicate it in other markets with your staff there, that is.

There is no shortage of Western examples of big brands that excel in one country and are terrible in another. I remember traveling in Europe and needing to buy an additional suitcase. I have a favourite brand to which I have been loyal over many, many years, and I wanted to buy another of their products. We were in Prague and arrived at the store a few minutes before 5:00 p.m. The lady running the store told us they were closing. I said all I wanted was one bag. Did she seem happy about the prospect of making an additional quick sale that day? No. Indeed, she walked over to the door and locked it in front of our faces with a very rude, angry expression, telling us she was closed.

In Japan, that type of customer service would be unthinkable. Having been here 33 years, I am fully tooled up for excellent, Japanese-style service. So, you can imagine the shock and horror that door-in-your-face treatment caused. I walked 100 metres up the road and bought the competitor's product. I couldn't understand that lady's negative attitude.

Having found that Prague has the cheapest, best beer I had ever enjoyed, I thought the entire country would be brimming with jolly, happy souls. Sadly, this was not the case in this particular retail endeavour.

To succeed here in Japan, you need to match what is required. You cannot allow your mind to be occupied with what you are used to, with what you grew up with. You can't imagine what the required levels of service would be. You have to come here and experience it. When you do that, you start to understand what you have to do back home to reorganize yourself to be able to service this market properly. That's easier said than done, though. The crew at home have no idea what you are talking about, because they can't imagine that level of service.

If you expect the Japanese buyer to adopt your standards, and to be satisfied with what you pass off as quality work, then you will be waiting a long time. It just won't happen.

In the next chapter, we will look at respect.

19—Respect

Respect in Japan may be more similar to concepts in European countries than in New World countries such as the United States and Australia. Age and stage probably carry more weight in older civilisations than in these bold new upstarts. In Japan, a low-ranking minion in a big company can have more status than the president of a small company. The president will show a lot more respect than what we would associate with the status of the person working for the bigger player. The individual has position power, purely on the basis of the company name. This is especially the case when the smaller company is a supplier. The small-company president will be very deferential to everyone in the buyer team, no matter their rank.

Inside large companies, there are many aspects of the power relationship that spill outside the corporate headquarters. Staff are living in subsidised company housing, and there is a complete hierarchy amongst the wives based on their husbands' ranks. Often, the section head's wife will be the Queen Bee, bossing the other wives around. I guess this is probably a bit like the military in many countries where families live on base. Rank and power are institutionalised in Japan, and we should understand that when we are here doing business.

Position power in Japan is often disconnected from actual personal capability. The higher-ranked person may, in fact, not be particularly competent, but they are shown respect anyway. In a country where you are promoted on the basis of age and stage rather than performance, this is bound to happen. In societies which have a performance-based system for moving up through the ranks, age counts for little in terms of respect. Actually, in youth-culture societies such as Australia, age is seen as a minus. Only the young know anything, and the elderly are not given much respect or credence. Codgers are considered over the hill and out-of-date. In our cultures, respect is shown for personal ability rather than age or stage.

Japan is the exact opposite. Here, the position itself is respected. Even if you are not shooting the lights out in terms of performance, people will still show respect because of the position you hold. The Japanese language even has polite honorific variations, called *keigo*, that are carefully calibrated to handle all these different levels of status. Get that wrong and there will be trouble.

When I was studying in Japan the first time in 1979, I was talking with an older lady who was a professor at my university. I wasn't using the correct *keigo* to respect her status above mine. Actually, at that time, I was happy to be able to string a sentence together in Japanese. How did I know I wasn't using the correct *keigo*? The way she replied to me, while absolutely correct, was dripping with ice and her body language joined in to school me on my impertinence. I knew immediately that I had said something the wrong way, even if I wasn't quite sure just what that was.

In business, Japanese buyers don't expect you to have any Japanese language skills, so if you try and are not using the correct honorifics, they won't be mortally offended like my good professor.

The truncation of ability and status in Japan means you have to keep your wits about you. If you are in a meeting and there are some younger, bright sparks there who are really engaging with you, don't ignore the older people sitting there saying very little. They will be senior, respected, and will be consulted. You can't ignore them, thinking you have the ear of the decision-makers. Be especially careful of giving the fluent English speakers too much credence. They are seen as language technicians by the hierarchy and often have no decision-making power at all.

If you are going to a meeting with the client, be respectful toward the receptionist. In the hierarchy between your two companies, she may rank above you. The young woman (and, in Japan, it usually is a young woman) who brings in the coffee or tea is another person you should show respect to. Do not imagine that you are some big shot from overseas, who is pretty important and can ignore the underlings like you do at home. In Japan, and actually everywhere, show respect for people doing their job regardless of their rank and what you perceive as their status power. You will have better success here if you do so, because it is noticed and noted.

Longevity is respected here, so someone who has spent their whole life devoted to the company is shown respect regardless of how capable they may be. By contrast, in the West, we are zigging and zagging our way up the ladder, trying to get to the big job. If you spend more than five years with a company, people begin to ask what is wrong with you. They wonder if you are a dud. If you had any ability, you would have moved to a higher position in another company by now.

That's not the case in Japan.

In the next chapter, we will look at longevity.

20—Longevity

Longevity means a lot in Japan. People who are risk averse like the fact that your company has been around for a long time. They know there is a certain degree of track record there. They sense that you are stable, predictable, credible, and reliable—all indicators that you are a low-risk choice of business partner. But if you are a new entrant, how does that work for you? You have no track record, no credibility, nothing to reduce the risk of having you as a supplier.

Your firm may be new to Japan, but perhaps it has an established track record in your own country. I previously ran an Australian bank here in Japan, and that company had been around for more than 150 years. We leveraged that track record to establish the levels of trust we needed here in Japan. When we advertised that the company had been founded in Australia, we used the Japanese imperial era system, rather than the Gregorian calendar, to emphasis our long history. That was how we used longevity to satisfy Japanese buyers.

In the case of Dale Carnegie Training, we always talk about the fact that we started 107 years ago in New York and 56 years ago in Japan. We do this to show that we are reliable and that potential clients can be confident about doing business with us. We are showing that we have stood the test of time.

Also, don't forget about yourself. If you have been with the same company for many years, don't neglect to mention that. It will be appreciated. It shows consistency, loyalty, and stability to the Japanese buyer. Japan is a not a country of job hopping. Unlike in most Western countries, where we bounce from job to job trying to step up our careers, here they go up the escalator and—over time—get to the top. Slow and steady wins the race. So, your steady career will look very familiar to them and it will correspond with what they think is a normal career progression.

In my case, I have been with Dale Carnegie Japan for 12 years, and I don't miss the chance to mention and highlight that. It shows commitment and, again, stability. Japanese companies want to have long-term relationships with people they can trust. Being a known factor is a big help in getting business done here. If I have already been with Dale Carnegie more than a decade, they know that I am not going anywhere and I will continue to be that known factor for them.

On the flip side of longevity is the fact that Japanese people love the new. When a new shopping mall opens here in Tokyo, the place is rushed with consumers going to check it out. They swarm like bees. After a few months, another new location will open and they will fly off and swarm there. This fascination with the new is a bit tricky and counterpoints longevity. So, here in Japan, we have a dual task. We need to highlight our stability and longevity while also being seen as something new and fresh. That is very important if you want to be relevant. We are a 107-year-old company, but we still have to make a big effort to innovate and release new Thought Leadership all the time. There is no resting on your laurels in Japan.

That is why I release three podcasts each week—*The Leadership Japan Series*, *The Sales Japan Series*, and *The Presentations Japan Series*. It is why I have my own YouTube TV Show, *The Cutting Edge Japan Business Show*, and why I publish two daily blogs—in English and Japanese—on Twitter, Facebook, and LinkedIn. And it is also why we have more than 800 free videos on our Japan Dale Carnegie TV YouTube channel. We have to show that we are fresh, current, and innovative, as well as being stable over time. What can you do to show that you have something new for buyers? There is strong demand here for new things. If you don't satisfy that demand, your competitor most likely will.

Another tricky part of longevity is keeping your contacts going. Large Japanese companies have a generalist model of executive development. You are an employee for life, and over your career will be rotated through all sections of the company. The idea is that you will gain a good appreciation of how the business works. The issue with this system is, come April 1 each year, the person you have been dealing with—and with whom you have built a solid relationship of trust—gets moved to a new job. Now there is a new person who may not know you, and may want to do their own thing or use their own trusted suppliers instead of you. You are now out.

This means that you have to keep in touch with companies. You can anticipate that changes will be made in April, so well before that you need to check in on your contact and find out what is likely to happen. Are they going to stay or will they be moved? If they are going to leave, then you want them to introduce you to their successor and try to weld the relationship firmly with the new person. Even if they have already made the move to another division, still get them to introduce you to their successor whenever possible. This will smooth the transition glide path considerably.

In the next chapter, we will look at crime.

21—Crime

C rime is a feature of any society. There are always going to be different elements of crime, activities that affect your personal safety. One of those is fraud, and it can come from outside and within your company.

Organised crime—the *yakuza*—are well established in Japan. They even have their own offices with their own shingle, announcing which gang they are. They are not as strong as they once were, but they are still a force. The chances of a foreign-run business having trouble with the *yakuza* is pretty low. For cultural and language reasons, they find dealing with us too hard. There are plenty of local Japanese they can exploit, and that is much easier.

They run prostitution, drug, and extortion rings. At various times, there have been media reports of a Japanese company president or employee being killed by *yakuza*, because they wouldn't pay them off or whatever. A new law introduced a few years ago that holds the gang boss responsible for the crimes of his underlings has had a strong negative impact on the yakuza; but they are still operating, and probably always will be.

You are more likely to run into *yakuza* in a club or bar. You are out on the town, you go for drinks, and are having a great time. When you get the bill, it is the equivalent of the gross national product of a medium-sized African country. You protest, and that is when the *yakuza chinpira*—or low-ranking punks—appear to persuade you to shut up and pay. And you had better pay.

If you go to places in Tokyo such as Roppongi or Shinjuku's Kabukicho, then you will be in *yakuza* territory and they will be running clubs and bars. If you get into any trouble with *yakuza* on the street, the safest place for you is at a *koban* (police box). Don't try to sort it out yourself. Get the cops involved. Anyway, you will have to work pretty hard to get yourself in trouble with the *yakuza* in Japan. It is very, very unlikely to ever happen.

Fraud is a different story. There are plenty of cases of Japanese people being taken to the cleaners through fraud. Japan has its share of Ponzi schemes. Often, they are pretty bad ones, in the sense that the perpetrators collect the money and then quickly disappear. They don't even bother to string it out over a number of years, as former stock broker Bernard Madoff did in the US. Here, they grab your cash and are then long gone.

You also hear anecdotal cases of a family's wealth having been stolen through business dealings with bad people. My Japanese wife's family and friends all know of cases in which a solid family has lost wealth through fraud from supposedly reliable business partners. So fraud does happen here.

If the deal sounds too good to be true, it is probably not something you want to be part of. There is no such thing as a free lunch in business. It is all hard work, hard work, hard work. At the start, it is very difficult to distinguish which business partners are the good guys and which are the crooks. Keep your wits about you.

Having said that, the chances of this happening are pretty slight. Again, all of those cultural and language issues make it hard for them to target you. And there are so many gullible Japanese *kamo* (targets) anyway, why waste time on the likes of you?

Counterintuitively, speaking Japanese can be a disadvantage in this regard. I was a *kamo* in a real-estate deal here and did lose a considerable sum of dough as a result. They had all the aces, as it turned out, and all I had was ignorance. But it was a strong lesson that due diligence is a must in Japan as well.

The other part of fraud is inside your own company. There is no shortage of cases of people stealing from banks, from their companies, etc. It does happen. In big companies, some staff are fabricating expense reports to get the cash for themselves. There was a case recently of a bank employee who was hiving off cash from some transactions he was involved in. Often, it is driven by bad gambling debts. The person becomes desperate to pay back the money, especially if they are dealing with the *yakuza*. Stealing from you sounds a lot better than getting beaten up or killed by the gang.

In the past, some of the short-term, high-interest cash-loan businesses would use *yakuza* muscle to collect the money. The usurious interest rates made it virtually impossible to ever clear the loan. That got cleaned up after a lot of scandals surfaced, but there is a lot of pressure to pay back the loan—so stealing from your employer starts to look like the only way out.

The other usual driver is the middle-aged married guy, trying to fund his young girlfriend's required lifestyle. He starts taking money from the company to make it all work. This can go on for years before it is finally discovered. Part of the reason is that Japan is such an honest culture that we all get lulled into a false sense of security. Have some mechanisms in place just to be on the safe side of the equation.

In the next chapter, we will look at buyer personality styles.

22—Buyer Personality Styles

We usually think in terms of cultural differences with the West when dealing with Japan. But it is differences in personality styles among buyers that is much more important. Cultural factors form a base, and on top of that are the idiosyncratic personality differences between Japanese buyers and ourselves. This becomes very key in communication. We won't be changing our personality style or that of the buyer any time soon, but we can vary our communication style.

For example, imagine a horizontal axis. On the far left are people who we would understand as having low levels of assertion. They do not state their opinion openly, they keep a low profile, and they spend much of their time watching what others are doing rather than doing it themselves. On the right side of the horizontal axis are people who are highly assertive. They state their opinion and seem to have an opinion on everything. They can be pushy, loud, and aggressive. When we meet someone for the first time, we can pretty much pick where they fall on this horizontal axis.

Now picture a vertical axis cutting through the middle of the horizontal axis. At the top of the axis are individuals with a strong people focus. They are very much interested in helping others, and are very concerned with how people feel. They often refer to the importance of people issues in their opinions and conversations. At the other end, at the bottom of that axis, are people who are focused on outcomes, results, and key performance indicators, or KPIs. They don't care as much about the people as they do about the results. They are totally focused on the numbers, and getting the numbers is all that counts.

If the buyer is on the high end of assertion and is driven by outcome, we call them a Driver personality type. This style transcends their Japanese cultural traits. They are much more direct than other Japanese. They are often the founder or owner of their own business. They are "time is money" types who don't care much about having a cup of tea with you. They want to get straight down to business, because they are always time poor and super busy.

When we are communicating with this type of person, we need to raise the volume of our voice and pump up the energy levels in our body language. We can get straight to the point with them, explaining what they should do and the three good reasons that makes sense. They are interested in how you can deliver results for them and little else. They don't want a relationship with you, they want outcomes. They will make a decision on the spot—without consulting anyone—and will then want to move on. This allows us to cut through a lot of the typical time-wasting to get to a consensus so they can make a decision. The downside is that they will just say no, and that is it. There is no going back to revisit the decision.

Their opposite number drives them nuts. These are the Amiables—those who are low in assertion and are people orientated. They are a sort of everyman type. As the name suggests, they want to have a cup of tea and get to know you before they will be happy to get into a business relationship with you. They speak quietly, display small amounts of energy or body language, and like to listen rather than do all the talking. They are slow to make a decision, because they need to make sure everyone is happy with what is going to happen. They are often the glue of the organization, going around to those who got sunburned by the Driver types in the meeting to make sure they are okay. Drop your voice and energy when you speak with them and emphasise how people will feel really good about the decision you are asking them to take.

The other assertive personality style is the Expressive. They are similar to the Driver, but have a greater people orientation. They tell jokes, smile a lot, have a lot of energy, and like to party. They are often salespeople, trainers, and actors. They like being around people, and they love the macro, the big picture. They grab the marker and are brainstorming on the whiteboard in a flash. They are thinking about the future, the vision, the great things that are to come. When with them, you should increase your energy and expect to be invited to parties, dinners, and events. Expressive types hate worrying about petty details—and just about all detail qualifies as petty for them. The typical salesperson hates filling out the CRM after the sales call, even though the marketing department is tonguing for the detail and data. Talk big picture with them and spare them the data and evidence. They don't have much interest.

Their opposite is the Analytical. These people are fine with three decimal places when dealing with numbers. They love detail, clarity, precision, evidence, testimonials, data, statistics, numbers, proof, etc. They are often accountants, doctors, engineers, scientists, and lawyers. Come armed with detail for them, as they cannot get enough of it. Don't ever worry that you will be maxing them out with data.

In the next chapter, we will look at praise and flattery.

23—Praise or Flattery

Japan is awash with praise, but it is praise more on the flattery side of the equation. When you get here, and you speak a few words of Japanese, people quickly tell you how fluent in Japanese you are. You use chopsticks at the restaurant and you get praised for mastering this tricky set of implements. This is all flattery, so don't believe a word of it. Japan has been a high-density living environment for thousands of years, so flattery is grease to smooth the wheels of societal interaction. The Japanese have learnt that the way to increase harmony is to smooth out all the rough edges, and this is where praise and flattery come in.

It happens in our countries, too. I am fascinated by American culture. Winston Churchill noted that the US and the UK are two countries separated by a common language. Australia and America look similar, but we, too, are quite different culturally. I was reminded of this recently when an American businessman whom I had just met for the first time at a networking event introduced me to another American businessmen by saying, "Come meet my good friend, Greg Story". No Australian would dream of doing that, because we are too cynical; but this is how they grease the wheels in America.

The difference with praise and flattery in Japan compared with the US, UK, and Australia is that the Japanese have institutionalised it. When you get praised in Japan, (a) don't believe a word of it, and (b) just politely accept it. Don't say, "No, no, no," when someone says something complimentary about you. Just politely say, "Thank you very much for saying that," and move on. Both sides will be happy with the fiction of the flattery.

Interestingly, because there is so much flattery going on here, you can cut through to them with some praise of your own. But you have to do it the right way. They all know it is flattery, so nothing really resonates. Everyone politely joins in the game of flattery and no one takes what is said at face value. You can have what you say taken at face value, however, if you know how to deliver the praise so it is believable. In that way, you can actually cut through and differentiate.

Be it the buyer, your team, or anyone you meet in Japan, if you want to recognise something they did, then be very specific about it. Don't make general comments like "very good" or "good job" or "good comment". All of this is too vague and just sits in the flattery basket, where it disappears almost immediately.

Instead, tell them something they did was good, but then isolate the thing that was good. So, with the case of a buyer, it might go like this: "Your comment in the meeting was really excellent. When you said that we should go together to visit your buyers, that was really insightful. I am sure those on the next level down never get visited, and the chance for us to meet them and say thank you is a great chance to build the relationship and increase future sales volumes. Thank you for bringing that possibility up at the meeting".

In this example, we have drawn out what was good, so that the praise is related to something specific they did which has value. If they are one of your staff members, tell them how what they did helps the firm's big picture. Encourage them to keep doing that and thank them once more.

If we just say, "Good job," they cannot relate to that comment, because they are doing many tasks. Just exactly which one are you referring to? We need to tell them, and it has to be genuine and true.

For example, we could say: "Suzuki-san, thank you for that great comment in the meeting. That was excellent. Your insight is very valuable. We are going to take that and change what we are currently doing to provide better service to the client, as a result of your comment, and this will help us win greater market share. It's thanks to you. We really appreciate that input. Please keep those insights coming, we really value you".

These examples will not be seen by the buyer or the staff members as simple flattery that can be disposed of and forgotten immediately. This style of praise will resonate and, in a country drowning in fake flattery, you will stand out in the crowd.

In the next chapter, we will look at asking questions of buyers.

24—Asking Questions of Buyers

In the West, we have all been trained in consultative selling for many decades. Buyers are used to salespeople turning up and asking a lot of questions to find out if there is some way they can help by providing their solution to solve the buyer's problems. The act of asking questions is never even thought about, because that is how it is done.

In Japan, there really aren't many professional salespeople. There are pitch people instead. They ask no questions. They just turn up and give their pitch. They roll out the flyers or the brochures and go straight into the nitty-gritty of the detail and the spec. They want to throw enough mud at the wall that some of it will stick. This is what the buyers have been trained to expect as well—no questions, just a pitchfest.

If you are coming out of the Western sales environment, you are going to be using consultative sales techniques and start asking the buyer a number of questions. This is a problem. In the West, we say the buyer is king. In Japan, the buyer is not king. They are God. By the way, God doesn't answer questions from impertinent salespeople. He or she is insulted by being asked questions. God gets the sales pitch and then destroys it, to make sure the risk factor has been fully minimized. That is the proper order of things here.

You can query the buyer in Japan, but you can't just blunder your way in there and start blasting forth with probing questions. Look at it from the Japanese buyer's perspective and put yourself in their place. How willing are you to share all the dirty little secrets of the firm with a total stranger whom you have just met? Get the idea of the problem we face?

You need to set it up first. Here is how.

Begin with a bit of chitchat to break the ice at the start of the meeting. Japan is very good at this. Next, describe what you do. Then, give an example of a similar company's case where you have helped them improve their results. Suggest that, "maybe", you could do the same for them. Next, say that, in order for you to know if that is a possibility, you need to ask a few questions. Would that be alright?

For example, "Dale Carnegie Training is a global specialist in soft skills training. We help people develop their careers and businesses to get the outcomes they are after. An example is XYZ company. We trained all of their hotel staff, and they found the client feedback really got a lift and that repeat bookings definitely increased. Maybe we could do the same for you. I am not sure, but for me to know if this is possible, would you mind if I asked you a few questions?". There is your request for permission to ask questions, as opposed to going straight into the questioning format.

You will notice that we say "maybe" we can do that for you rather than definitely we can. In the West, we might say, "We can definitely do this for you". We would make it a confident statement. But in Japan, we say "maybe". We do this to make it soft and less aggressive. We only request permission to ask a few questions. If there is no match, well, there won't be many questions. But if there is a match—and there is interest—there may in fact be many questions. We won't know until we ask the first few questions of the buyer.

We ask well-designed questions of the buyer and are simultaneously mentally running through our library of solutions to see if we can help. If we can't, we shouldn't be wasting their time. We should move on and find a buyer we can actually help.

When it comes to the solution provision part, we know what they were after. So, usually, we can link our product or service to the solution provision they need. In Japan, it doesn't work like that. The pitch person here turns up and skips straight past the questioning stage and plunges headlong into the detail of the solution. They do this not even knowing if it is the appropriate solution. The buyer has been trained by these pitch people and is simply not able to encompass the concept of questions for God. This is the lay of the land.

Then you turn up with your professional Western sales approach and start asking questions straight away. What you get from the buyer is total silence—they just don't respond. Remember, this is because they can't accept God being questioned by a nobody. They will just change the subject and ask for your pitch. Trust me, you don't want to go there if you want to make a sale.

You have to set things up and get permission to ask questions. If you do that, you will be successful in Japan. If you want to be a pitch person instead, let me know how that is working out for you. I don't think it will go too well. Much better to be a professional salesperson and ask well-designed questions to uncover where you can be of service to the buyer. Remember, when questioning buyers in Japan, get permission first.

In the next chapter, we will look at explaining the application of the benefits to buyers.

25—Explaining the Application of the Benefits to Buyers

J apan loves data and detail. All good, but it can be a trap when you are here trying to make sales. In a Western sales model, there is a defined process to go through, and the buyer is also trained on how that works. In the Japanese case, there is a bit of a love of detail bias, and this will take you down the wrong path if you let the buyer control the sales call—and that happens to all the Japanese salespeople here, by the way.

The buyer loves the detail, the spec, and the features of the product. They can't get enough of that stuff. The problem is, we don't buy the features; we buy the outcomes of the benefits. In sales training, we often use the example of buying a hand drill at a DIY centre. There are tonnes of detail on the drill, such as the weight, speed, power source, colour, and battery life. But we are not buying a drill. What we are really buying is a hole of a certain size, in brick, metal, concrete, or wood. The drill's features are not the end goal, but that is often all the salesperson talks about.

So, here in Japan, we have to be careful. The buyer can drag us down into the morass of details and features if we are not careful. We must control the sales call and redirect the conversation away from the details and specs to the outcomes and benefits these features will provide for the buyer. Generally speaking, most salespeople around the world get to the feature bit while only a tiny minority elevate the conversation to cover the consequent benefits of those features. Japanese pitch people have trained the buyers here to focus on the spec, the detail, the data, the micro elements.

We need to get to a higher level of discussion. We need to be drawing word pictures the buyer can see in their mind's eye. We need to be describing all the benefits they will get from this purchase. This requires telling stories, talking about outcomes and results.

Having done that, we need to show evidence that what we say works really does. The series of statements coming out of the salesperson's mouth is not counted as evidence. Salespeople like to talk—a lot. We can do this, we can do that, or we have this or that. So what? We need to be referring to the cases where we have helped other companies. We need to provide data to back up what we are saying. We need to be showing the application of the benefits and where this has worked elsewhere. This makes the whole sales call more credible.

This has to be real. You cannot make this stuff up. If you want to lie to the buyer, then get out of the sales profession; the rest of us don't want you polluting the waters. It has to be authentic and real—something that you can prove to the buyer if they want that level of detail. Then you have to move into a trial close to see if there are any areas of concern. Is there something we haven't covered in sufficient detail? Did we miss anything? Are there any objections to what we have said?

The Japanese pitch person doesn't get to any of this sophistication. They are bogged down in the detail of the features. Remember, the buyer has been trained to only expect the pitch. They will keep you there and keep asking detailed micro questions. They do this because they are risk averse and want to make sure there will be no issues with your solution. That is fine, but we can't stay there for the whole sales call. You have to move them out of the minutiae and up the ladder to the next sunny uplands of benefits, application of those benefits, evidence that the solution works, and a trial close. This is a structure. Sadly, the Japanese pitch person doesn't have any structure whatsoever except hoping for good luck to land a deal.

We need to reeducate buyers in Japan on selling. We have to guide them along a different path from the one they are used to. It isn't easy, but, if you want to make sales in Japan, it is a requirement.

In the next chapter, we will look at handling buyer objections.

26—Handling Buyer Objections

Y ou would expect that salespeople would hear a lot of objections from buyers—particularly the same objections—and therefore would be pretty good at handling them? Well, that actually isn't the case. Sometimes, foreign salespeople imagine they can drive the process by force of will and by pushing the buyer to change their mind. This is ridiculous anywhere, but especially here in Japan. Or they want to argue with the buyer, outmanoeuvre them, outwit them, somehow trick them into buying. Again, ridiculous.

Japan has a very risk averse culture, and the objections are important to the buyer to get a surety of making a low-risk buying decision. They are salaried employees who don't want to see any decision they make come back to haunt them. The easiest way to prevent that is to take no new decisions (like buying from you).

An objection is like the headline in a newspaper. It is very concise, but there is a long article explaining what that headline is all about. When we hear that headline, we need to get the full story to be able to deal with the objection. There is no point in hearing the objection and then answering what you second-guess the real point may be. It is a bit like at school, when you get the essay topic and write your answer only to discover that is not what the teacher was after. We have to be sure of what the buyer is after before we attempt to answer the objection. Don't answer what you think the problem might be. Ask them.

I was at an event recently, sitting next to a Japanese sales director, and I asked how he handled objections. His answer nearly had me falling off my chair in shock. He said that, whenever he meets an objection, he drops the price by 20 percent. I was mentally calculating what that meant, because he had told me there were 10 salespeople in the team. Ten people dropping the price by 20 percent every year for five years amounts to a diabolically large number. There is no need for that, I told him.

He was dropping the price because he didn't know what else to do. What he should have been doing was questioning the objection?

He should have been asking the buyer why they held their view? If they said the price is too high, he needed to ask them why they thought so.

In another example, I had that exact reaction from a client. When I questioned why they thought the price was too high, they said it was because the amount exceeded their budget allocation for training for that quarter. So, I asked if it would make a difference if we spread that investment over two quarters. They said, yes, that would be fine. The real objection was timing, not price, but I would never have known that if I had just dropped my price by 20 percent.

Also, when people give their objection, we have to be thinking, "Is this really the objection?" It is like the iceberg metaphor. What they say is like the bit above the waterline, but the real objection is out of sight, underwater. We do this ourselves when we are out shopping. We see a nice suit, check the price, and take a deep breath because it is too expensive for us. When the clerk asks us about buying the suit, we don't say, "Well, I have been too unsuccessful so far in my career to afford an expensive suit like this one". No, we talk about the bit above the waterline—we don't like the colour or the pattern or whatever. But that is not the real reason.

So, when we get an objection, we need to keep asking if there are any other points until we have flushed out some of the issues. We then ask the buyer to rank these issues in order of priority. The most pressing objection is the one we answer. Often, all the others disappear once we handle the main one.

If the objection is a game-breaker, then that is it. You can't force them to buy. Badgering won't help. Leave that sales call and go spend time with someone who you can properly serve. Don't waste your most valuable resource: time.

Don't argue with the buyer. They may not be the buyer today, but one day they may buy. Leave the door open. You may find that you can do a deal in the future, so don't burn your bridges over one deal.

In the next chapter, we will look at closing sales.

27—Closing Sales

You would think that asking for the order would be the simplest thing in a sales job. Not the case in Japan. Surprisingly a lot of salespeople here never ask directly for the order. They get to the point where they should ask, but they choose not to.

One of the reasons is they fear rejection, getting a "no". The job of sales is an emotional rollercoaster—no matter where you are in the world—so preserving your self-esteem and self-belief is critical. There is nothing like getting rejected when selling to knock your ego around. By not actually asking for the business, Japanese salespeople have found a way to avoid that regretful eventuality. The proposition is left vague, sort of hanging there.

They lack skills in selling, so the steps which they should have completed in a professional manner haven't been done. And so they have no right to ask for the order. If you have built the trust, asked well-designed questions to fully understand the client's needs, presented the correct solution, and dealt with any hesitations or objections, then you can confidently ask for the order.

The way of asking doesn't have to be aggressive or a hard sell. In fact, that won't work in Japan, so let's forget about that idea. We can ask simply, "Shall we go ahead?" Or, we might offer an alternative of choice, such as, "Would you like to start in July, or would August be better?" Choosing either of those months means that they are accepting the business and will go ahead with the deal. Another soft variation that works well in Japan is to use a minor point. We can ask, "Shall I send you a hard copy of the invoice or is an electronic copy okay?" Either answer means "Yes, we have an agreement".

Most often in Japan, the answer is "We need to discuss it" or "We need to think about it". In American sales training, they have a harder edge and go after that statement, "What do you need to think about ..." or "How long will you take to ...". That type of pushy sales technique just won't work in Japan.

Here, they do have to think about it. They also have to discuss it. The person you are talking to is usually neither the final nor sole decision maker. They must follow the *ringi seido* system, in which all the stakeholders have to attach their *chop* (personal stamp) to the recommendation to show they have been informed and they agree. That means a lot of internal consultation is required, so it is hard to make any commitments to the salesperson immediately. No manner of bullying the buyer is going to change that situation.

We have to be thinking how we can help our champion sell the idea to the other colleagues. We have to provide the arguments and show the value to make their persuasion job easier. We also need to find out who the primary people are. Who inside the company must be convinced? And what issues might be important to them? Knowing these things, we can help our champion address any potential push-back that might occur behind the closed doors of the client company.

We need to ask for the order to flush out any objections we may not have dealt with well enough in the earlier part of the sales cycle. Maybe we didn't do a good enough job designing questions to fully understand the needs of the buyer. Maybe our solution wasn't a good enough match for what they needed. Perhaps we didn't handle the objections which arose well enough. Sometimes the objections we were told were just a smokescreen, and the real objections haven't emerged yet. We need to get these out if we are to deal with them. If we don't ask for the order, we won't get the business—and we won't find out why we are not getting the business.

If they do bring up an issue, don't fight it. Say: "Yes, I see. And why is that a problem for you?" Any answer you start with words such as "no", "but", or "however", will be guaranteed to have the buyer stop listening and go into combat mode, ready to argue. We need to ask them why this an issue to get more detail on the table so that we can deal with it. If we can't deal with it, then don't waste any more time. Get out there and find the next potential client.

When closing in Japan, do not use aggression, force of will, or tricky closing techniques. None of that will work. Use soft sell here. Expect that the buyer will need to think about it, so we must be prepared to help them sell the idea internally.

In the next chapter, we will look at follow up.

28—Follow-up

There are two elements of follow-up in Japan. One is when you have concluded the deal and it is time to affect the delivery of the service or product. Prior to that, there has usually been a long, drawn-out process during which the buyer side have "been thinking about it". Actually, they have been thinking about it because they need to get consensus internally on whether or not they should do the deal. They are trying to ensure they have minimised any risk, that they have all the checks and balances in place. This can take a lot of time, and it is very frustrating for the seller.

However, when they have finally gotten everyone on board, they strike the deal and then expect everything to be done by yesterday. The demand for speed in execution is always there in Japan. In the West, we tend to be the polar opposite. We are fast to strike a deal, then slow to deliver. Be aware: in Japan, once the gun goes off, things must already be primed to spring into action. That means we must have the logistics side of our delivery ready to go—and at speed.

The other element of follow-up is a bit trickier. We have lots of meetings with clients. One side is thinking about the proposed deal while we keep seeking out new clients. We can't sit around waiting for a decision; we have to keep moving forward. This leads to a problem: we lose touch with people we spoke to some time ago, because we have moved on. We are looking for the next potential deal and keep adding these potential deals to the list.

We need to have a good system of follow-up. The buyer said they would think about it and we need to set a cadence for the follow-up to see how they are progressing internally. We need to work out the frequency of follow-up. That requires a good tracking system for clients we have met but who have not yet bought from us.

Buyers also benefit from the follow-up because they drift, too. After they have met us, they get swept up in work as well, and trying to get people together internally to discuss the arrangements can take time. So, the buyer also gets distracted. Remember, it is very rare that the buyer will ever experience any urgency about purchasing anything.

As the volume builds, the capacity for our memory to deal with all the complexity is challenged. This is where client management systems and alert systems are needed. We have to set this up to help us keep up with all the many things we are doing. Someone you met six weeks ago may be a distant memory, and you can barely remember what you talked about. What is worse, you have become totally distracted by clients who you are talking to now, and you have not been doing a good job keeping in touch with that buyer from six weeks ago as they slowly work their way through the deliberation process.

It happens pretty easily, if you are busy working on leads. As an example, in just a two-day period this week, I had a lunchtime networking event, another one that evening, then one at breakfast the next day, and finally another luncheon after that breakfast. I collected a wad of *meishi* (business cards). Some of these can just be filed in our CRM system, but others need to be contacted to arrange a meeting. So, you send off the email asking to get together. The trick today, though, is that nobody answers your email and nobody is ever there to answer your follow-up call. These people go into the Bermuda Triangle of Sales Follow-up. They disappear. Unless we have a good system of dealing with all of this, we will be wasting a lot of energy and missing opportunities to do more business.

So, follow-up in Japan has its own peculiarities, and we have to be ready to deal with them. Speed in response to a "go" decision—and keeping in touch with potential buyers through the long journey to a "yes"—is absolutely required for success here.

In the next chapter, we will look at worry.

29—Worry

We face many worries in business in Japan. Cash flow would have to be the biggest. Run out of cash and you are gone. Do we have a good balance between serving established clients and finding new clients? Expense control means making sure the fixed-costs line is kept as low as possible, which isn't that easy in Japan.

Then we have to worry about taking care of our people. We know that hiring people to replace those who leave is a difficult job, and it is not likely to get any easier. We have to recruit new staff, but, more importantly, we need to retain our existing staff. We must keep the young people engaged and away from that grass which is supposedly greener on the other side of the fence.

For the older team members, there are health issues and also the issues around taking care of ageing parents. This part of our workforce faces a lot of stress. We can't afford to lose them, and this whole issue of people working longer will only grow as society ages and the workforce shrinks. Along with it will come a new range of concerns that we didn't have to worry about much in the past.

How flexible are we about working conditions? With the young people, we are in the free-agent era and they are totally mobile, because they can easily get another job. They enter companies, and when the glamorous image meets reality they start to look toward the door. This is a cost to us, and we see them go to our competitors, which is extremely painful.

What do we do about all these worries? Often the worry is like observing 100 butterflies at the same time. We can't really focus on one of them, because the whole scene is constantly moving. Worries tend to be the same problem: they are floating around and we have a hard time pinning them down. We know we have to do something, but we are becalmed. We just can't see where to start.

We need to isolate the worst thing that could happen. Get very clear on what that would be. Call it out. This, in itself, is very important. Rather than dealing with vague, subconscious worries, we name it and elevate it to front of mind.

Next, we have to say to ourselves mentally that it will happen, it will occur. We can't be in denial, we have to be realistic and say that it is going to happen—the worst thing possible is going to happen to us. Again, this is calling it out big time, really confronting the ogre in the room.

Having faced that down, we now get thinking about what we can do to lessen the degree of catastrophe about to unveil itself. What are the options to lessen the impact of the blow. We can see it coming, and we may not be able to avoid it, but that doesn't mean we are totally helpless. What can we salvage? What opportunities does this throw our way that otherwise would never have revealed themselves? What is the best option amongst the many we have thought about? Some won't be so realistic or practical, some will be half-formed ideas, and some will no doubt never be taken up. But after listing them and thinking about them, some will have value and potential. We need to get out of our self-induced immobilisation and get a plan together of the steps we need to take.

The actions we take may not work immediately, but now we are in action mode as opposed to paralysis mode. We can redirect our energies, alter the plan, refine the plan, scrap the plan, and start again. A start is a start, and momentum invites further momentum. Doing all this from our action mode is much easier than sitting around saying, "Woe is me, what will I do?" We can bury ourselves in self-pity or we can get off our backside and try and fix the issue. This is all easy to say, but when your mind is in a fog it is hard to see a way forward. So, start with the smallest thing and this will lead to other things happening. Eventually you will be steamrolling forward to a solution.

In the next chapter, we will look at stress.

30—Stress

Today, we all know that stress is a killer. Stress is something that sits there under the surface and affects our health and performance. It runs deep and can well up inside us. We are not fixing it or diminishing it. Japan can be a very stressful place in business. Decisions take a long time, and the client is never on your timetable. Your expected payment didn't turn up on time. You discover that the invoice had to be in by the 15th of the month, but no one bothered to tell you that, so you are not getting paid until the next month and now cash flow issues are arising.

Currency movements have had a strong impact on your profitability, and this wasn't factored in fully when you created the business plan. Regulatory barriers are making it hard to supply the market. Buyers prefer the devil they know to the angel they don't—and that means you. So, how do you break into this market when nobody knows you? Then you have the problems of running your own team. People are getting older and have all sorts of personal health issues, or issues around taking care of their parents. You have issues recruiting and retaining younger staff. The list just goes on and on.

What do we do about all this? There are many things blinding us to the real issues. We are battling through a fog of confusion most of the time. We have to cut through that and work out clearly just what is the problem. Unless we can identify the problem, we have little hope of fixing it.

This isn't as easy as it sounds, because there could be many factors at play. Which are the really key ones? The simple breakthrough here is to write them down. Somehow, the act of writing helps us to refine what we are thinking. We then need to put those factors in order of priority. That forces a higher level of thinking about what we are facing. Are there any threads and similarities?

Having sorted that bit out, we now have to dig a bit deeper and look at the causes behind these problems. We can identify the symptoms, but what are the root causes of the troubles we are suffering. This again needs some analysis, and often we are not operating with a lot of numbers we can rely on to pick out the threads of the root causes. We have to go on instinct, and that is an imperfect science.

So, we have ascertained the cause of the problem. Great! But what can we do about it? We start digging deep for solutions, for ideas, for innovations which will provide us with a way forward. This is a brainstorming process, and the object should be to come up with as many ideas as possible. We do this on the basis that even a crazy, impractical idea might be the trigger for a really fantastic idea. The truly excellent idea may not have emerged without the stimulus of the crazy idea in the first place.

Having drawn out a broad range of possibilities, we now need to whittle these down to the best ideas. We start evaluating the consequences of taking possible actions. We distil the best solution in this way, and create a roadmap for ourselves. Through action comes clarity, and the solutions flow forth. We need to get the battle plan into priority order for the execution piece. We are trained in business to execute, and once we get a plan together we can start to move forward and get out of the hole we have been lodged in for some time.

Dale Carnegie wrote a whole book on this subject called *How to Stop Worrying and Start Living*. He was thinking that we needed to find a way through the worry stage and get out of that pit we have dug for ourselves. Once we do that, we get on the front foot and can exercise more control over our attitude and circumstances. This means we can start living in a full and complete way, because we have thrown off the yolk of worry and are now tapping into our full potential.

If you find alcohol isn't doing it for you, or you find yourself worrying while at yoga, maybe get the book and read it. Today, we know the connection between stress and illness—and we can't take it lightly.

In the next chapter, we will look at time.

31—Time

T ime is life, time is money, and time is your business. In Japan, business decisions are made at a glacial pace, but buyer expectations for your response and follow-through are exceedingly high.

Tokyo, especially, bustles along. You see it in the mornings. I catch my subway train around 7:15 a.m. and, to my astonishment, I see people professionally dressed for business, running through the subway station. I ask myself why on Earth are they running at 7:15 in the morning? Who knows, but it just reinforces that things are moving fast here in this crazy capital. The pace of life is rapid, so we have to be very well organised to keep up with buyer's expectations.

It is so much harder to be well organised these days. Emails are hitting our inboxes like a tsunami—wave upon wave of new messages—without remorse and without relent. You cannot call anyone anymore, because they are in meetings. Everyone is in meetings. You know your email will get drowned in their inbox—and you cannot get them on the phone—so making contact with people in business is so much harder than it was in the past. I thought all these cool tech innovations we have today would make business easier, but that is not necessarily the case. Our windows to people are getting narrower and our time openings more compressed. So, we have to become like demons on speed when it comes to better organizing ourselves.

One important aspect of that is planning our day. Now, some people reading this may be thinking: "Forget that! I am a free spirit! I am going to do it my way. I don't want to be bound by rules and schedules. I need the muse to come out and I want to run my business that way". I very much doubt you are operating at maximum performance with such an approach. The cold, hard reality is that we have to plan our days extremely efficiently, because we are all so time poor.

Other people may be thinking: "Yeah, yeah, I know all that. I know I have to prioritise my day". It reminds me of my 18-year-old son, who, whenever I tell him to do something, says, "Yeah, yeah, Dad, I know", but then doesn't do it. We all know what we should be doing, but it doesn't mean we actually get around to doing it.

What should we be doing? We should be seeing our time management in holistic, whole-of-life terms. There is no point just planning for business, because your life is so multifaceted and there are many areas apart from work which need attention.

We play more than just a business role in our lives. I am a husband, father, colleague, leader, salesman, writer, perpetual student, friend, and an investor, among many other things. Every one of these roles has priorities which must not be sacrificed just for the business component. We need to work out what our respective roles are and plan our goals and priorities for each. That old saw about "nobody on their deathbed wished they had spent more time down at the office" is true. The way to make sure that doesn't happen is to have specified goals for all aspects of your life, organized in order of priority.

When it comes to daily planning, we draw on these goals and make sure that all priorities—business and otherwise—are covered off. The classic example is that you are too busy working in your business to get your personal taxes done on time, or to get your expense claims completed. This is when you know that you have a failed time-management system in place. Japan is good in that regard, as the tax department here does not brook any late filings or extensions, so you have to get it done or else!

Start with your goals and review the priorities you have set. Then see if any of these need to be injected into today's schedule. This will capture both business and non-business objectives. Calling your aged parents every week should be in there. Spending time to watch your kids play sports should be in there. Reading about investment information should be in there. Getting your tax submission documentation should be in there.

The point is, your life is multifaceted, so your goals and priorities should be also when you are planning your schedule. This then gets boiled down to a daily to-do list, organised in order of greatest import. Which one of these many things is the most urgent or will have the greatest impact? Start with that one. This is key. You have to start with the highest-priority item and stick with it—unless something happens that forces you to rearrange the order.

Here is the main takeaway: you cannot do everything, but you can get the most important thing done every day. If you can do that, you will be so far ahead of everyone else it will be ridiculous. I sometimes fail in this regard, and I lack the discipline to do things in the order of highest priority. I don't think I said I was a saint, did I? Anyway, the key is to try. I know myself that the days I do manage it are so vastly more efficient than the days I don't. The evidence is overwhelming that being better organised around goals and priorities—and having the discipline to compete tasks in order—leads to greater success.

In the next chapter, we will look at delegation.

32—Delegation

We know that delegating tasks is important, but we have tried it in the past and found that it didn't work particularly well. So, we have given up on it. Why didn't it work well? Usually it is because of the way we do the delegation. We just dump the task on someone and tell them when we want it, as we gracefully slide off into the mist. We turn up at the designated production point to find it hasn't been done, or it has errors, or it has been taken off in a completely different direction from what we expected. And now it is too late to fix it by the deadline. We blame "delegation"—the process—rather than ourselves and our delegation methodology.

So, we start saying dumb things to ourselves like, "It would be faster if I do it myself". We do this because we don't want to invest the time in teaching someone else how they should be doing it. This is a big mistake, because if we keep doing it this way, we will never be able to delegate anything. There is a big opportunity cost here, because we can't free up the time we need to work on the high-level things that only we can work on.

Just dumping work on others builds resentment. Clever people in Japan have worked out that, if they do a poor job, they can't be fired, and the boss will buy back the delegation. This way, they will never have to worry about a recurrence. If you ask Japanese people to write out their job description, they can fit it on the back of a postage stamp. The reason is that they want to reduce their work responsibility to the smallest possible scope. They are highly risk averse, and the narrower the scope of responsibility the less chance of having any egg wind up on their faces. Pretty smart, really.

Then we turn up with our shiny idea to give them more work. They think they are too busy already and don't have any bandwidth for more tasks. Also, you are expanding their risk circle rather than reducing it. From their point of view, there is nothing to like about doing tasks that are the boss's responsibility, rather than theirs. They see nothing in it for them.

Okay, then how should we delegate? We need to persuade people to do the task willingly. The first step is to match the task to the best person, rather than to whomever doesn't look that busy that day. Next, we need to sell the idea to them. We have to speak in terms of how it will benefit them. It is hard to move up the ranks, usually because of a lack of experience at the next level. Delegation is an excellent way for an aspiring worker to get notches in their belt through the practical experience of doing tasks at the boss's level. When they get to the interview stage for their next job—or when discussing a promotion—they can talk about how they have completed tasks at the boss's level already. That helps the person making the decision on a hire or promotion to be sure they can do the job.

We need the person to whom we have delegated the task to lead the project planning. "We own the world we help to create," so let them create the plan of execution. Of course, we can help, but it shouldn't be our plan rammed down their throat. They may actually have a better way of doing it than what we had thought of.

Let them run with it, but check on the way through. There is a fine line here with checking and micromanaging, but we have to be careful to keep the responsibility with them. We need to check that the task is on track with what we agreed—and that is all we should be doing. Let them do it. Finally, we celebrate their successful completion of the project.

In the next chapter, we will look at handling mistakes.

33—Handling Mistakes

Mistakes happen. The important thing is how we handle them—especially in Japan. How do you handle mistakes by your staff? We want innovation, we want improvement, we want people stepping out to grow the business. The problem in Japan is that making a mistake is taken very seriously. Bosses will berate staff for errors, and colleagues will be less than supportive. Consequently, staff have learned to avoid all possibility of making a mistake by not taking any risks and by dodging all additional responsibility and accountability.

We want the opposite, but the problem is that people are reluctant to take a chance. When mistakes happen, everyone is watching to see how the boss will react and handle the problem. They are all thinking, "What will happen to me if I make a mistake?" When they see their colleagues being hauled over the coals, they judge that this is something to avoid. The best way to escape the wrath of the boss is to keep doing the same old safe things and not try anything new.

So, we need a philosophy and methodology for handling mistakes. Do you have one? Here are some ideas. Firstly, we should check the facts of what happened and not be led by hearsay. Once we have the details and are sure they are correct, we need to engage the person who was responsible for the mistake. How do you habitually approach the mistake-maker? Do you confront them with the sordid details of their crime and rebuke them?

Another way, which will work much better, is to refer to the mistake indirectly. Keep the confrontational nature of the conversation to a minimum. By referring to the mistake indirectly, we allow people to keep face and to more easily volunteer the information about what happened. The confrontational approach tends to breed denial.

Another way might be to talk about our own mistakes. We might refer to a time in our career when we got it wrong and explain what happened. We do this to show that we understand that we all make mistakes, and that it is a very human thing. It is also a subtle reminder that mistakes are not fatal. Here you are, now the boss, despite having tripped up in the past.

It is going to be very rare that a person won't know they erred. They will know it, and they will be feeling bad, guilty, and shy about having let the team down. We need to keep that in mind and approach the conversation very gently.

Their confidence will have gone right down, and they will be locked away in their comfort zone, afraid to come out. We need to counter that feeling and restore their confidence. We should lure them out of their comfort zone so that they can contribute to the firm's future. We can explain that the innovation process is a messy thing and that mistakes will happen, and we accept that part of the trade-off with getting people to try new things is to allow for errors. If it is a straight-up error that has nothing to do with innovation, then we need to have a different conversation about precision and double-checking.

When we get to the next stage, we ask the person what we can do to recover. Now, would you normally start correcting them and telling them what to do? To engage their ideas and insights instead, you might try asking them for help with what to do. In this way, they feel in control and will have a strong sense of ownership of the solution. As we have noted, people own the world they help to create, so we should let them do just that. This also means that the execution piece is more likely to be done well by them, because it is their idea. Let them work out some possible solutions, select the best ones, and get the person busy on fixing the problem.

On the other side, if they totally deny any responsibility, if they are not being cooperative, then we have a different type of problem. Taken to the extreme, we will have to reconsider if we want someone who refuses to take responsibility and be accountable working with us.

Remember, this denial approach is driven by fear. They are worried that they will be fired for the mistake. They don't expect to be recruited to fix it. This is the risk-averse nature of Japanese culture at play. We need to assure them that this mistake will not result in a life sentence or capital punishment. They need to know that they may suffer some penalties for the error, but they can recover and keep going with their career. But, first, they have to take responsibility for what they have done.

If we are able to do it this way, others who are watching won't be spooked by innovative ideas or change. They will see that this is a culture of coming out of the comfort zone and trying things. They will see that people are valued and not thrown by the wayside at the first sign of trouble. The group expects them to take responsibility and also that people are treated humanely by management.

In the next chapter, we will look at celebrating wins.

34—Celebrating Wins

We imagine we are celebrating our wins. But are we really? I think about myself and realize, I am not doing it. This is a good reminder for myself that I should be celebrating more often. Japan is a highly risk averse culture, so when we ask people to step out of their comfort zone, they hesitate. Most people don't like change, so there needs to be encouragement to do so and recognition of the effort. Avoiding risk, responsibility, and accountability are gold medal-winning traits on the part of most Japanese people. This is their risk-averse nature coming through.

We are all looking for innovation and progress, and that means doing things we aren't automatically good at. It means mistakes and possible failures. All of these things get penalized in Japan. No wonder people like doing the same and safe routines they are familiar with. We have to think about how to reward people for stepping up and stepping out.

That means praise, recognition, and celebrating wins—however small—at the start. This isn't like Christmas, where we only get presents once a year. We shouldn't be saving up for just a celebration at the end of the financial year. We need to be doing more of that along the way, throughout the year. Are you?

Now, I am a shocker in this regard. I am the classic example of Protestant work ethic—a go, go, go type of guy. Sometimes I look at my diary and say, "Great! No meetings tomorrow". Then I realize this is because it is a public holiday. I have been so totally focused on the work and have forgotten all about the holiday. I am self-contained, self-motivated, and independent, so I don't need anyone to tell me anything. Well, that might be fine for me, but that is not the case for everyone. Other people want praise, recognition, and the feeling of being appreciated. I am certainly not the model.

As the leader, I have to keep telling myself that others are different. They need motivation, they need that supportive environment, with praise and conversations. This is particularly the case when we are trying to grow people's comfort zones. They need help to make the changes needed to grow their abilities. This means we recognize the smallest progress, because change is hard for everyone.

We have to make it easy for people to change, and that means creating a smooth glide path to help them on the way through. That means not waiting until the end of the year to have a big celebration. We hit the target, so we celebrate. We missed the target, so the party is cancelled. It doesn't work like that, because people need help all the way through the year to get to the result we all want.

So, if you are a hopeless workaholic like me, then designate someone else as the party organiser, to set the party dates and create the event. Make it happen around you—or even in spite of you—rather than needing it to come from you. If you are like me, in that case, there will never be any parties or celebrations, just more work. Make sure the delegatee is executing on this. Our job should just be checking on the progress. Hard work is fine, but many people want the collegial atmosphere, they want to have the camaraderie, they want to let off some steam together.

Actually, I have a confession. This whole conversation and topic is, for me, to remind me to celebrate the small wins, to get other people doing it on my behalf so that, in fact, it gets done. I hope you find this reminder of "do what I say, rather than what I am doing" helpful. I promise to do better on the win celebration front!

In the next chapter, we will look at two critical Japanese cultural contexts: *tatemae* and *honne*—the public face and the real face.

35—*Tatemae* and *Honne*: Public Face and Real Face

"Japanese are two-faced". This is a common reaction to a major cultural difference with the West. Someone says one thing but does something else or—more often than not—doesn't do what they said they would do. This is where the "two-faced" accusation arises.

You make a presentation. They tell you it is very good and that they will study it carefully. Your expectations are high, because you feel you are on the brink of an agreement and the money will start flowing your way very shortly. Everyone was so nice, smiley, and friendly. You feel you established some solid rapport with the buyer group. Japanese people are so polite, you are thinking.

You never hear from them again. When you email them to follow-up, there is no response. When you call them back, they are always away from their desk in a meeting. The person who answers says, "Call them back later" (never volunteering the idea you could leave your number for them to call you back). You do call them back and, lo and behold, get the same routine as before.

This time you have wised up a bit, so you cleverly give them your number and ask that they call you back. The person you are talking with assures you they will pass on the number, and that your call will be returned. But it never is. They have now disappeared into the great void and you are wondering what on earth happened. Everyone seemed so positive. They said they would study it. Now they have spurned your every attempt to follow up.

This scenario plays out all the time here in different guises, but with the same outcome. You are told something and then it doesn't occur. You feel betrayed. What is going on?

We need some context. Japan is the world champion in managing high-density living in great harmony, and has done so for many, many centuries. For example, the contrast to the trash heaps masquerading as major cities in Europe in earlier times— with sewage flowing in open drains and trash being thrown in the streets—couldn't be greater. Japanese cities were, and still are, clean. Everyone cleans up around their house or place of business. You will always see shopkeepers cleaning up the street in front of their store and, in summer, spreading water to keep down the dust. You don't see any of this in the West.

We had World Clean Up Day here the other day and my team participated. It was a joke, really, because the streets here are so pristine. We struggled to find any garbage to pick up. We got the obligatory group photo though! It has been like this for a long time. What this means is that, even centuries ago, Japan had clean cities achieved through mutual, interlocking responsibilities. They didn't have the same levels of personal confrontation that Western urban inhabitants had.

The Japanese have worked out that living together cheek by jowl requires the suspension of some absolute truths, and these have been replaced with relative ones.

This flexibility with the truth is what drives the charge of being two-faced. They will tell you something you want to hear, knowing full well they can't do it, just to keep everything harmonious and avoid any ugly confrontations. You ask someone on the street where some place is located, they point you in the opposite direction to which they are going, and, about 20 minutes later, you say to yourself, "Wait a minute, they have sent me in the completely wrong direction!" Actually, they didn't know the location themselves, so to avoid the embarrassment of admitting that, they sent you in the direction where you were most unlikely to ever meet them again, should you discover the truth.

You may have had a really good business meeting and your hopes are high. Maybe your point person there actually did their best for you to get the deal approved, but internally the decision went the other way. They won't be doing any business with you. Having met you, that would be an embarrassing conversation that would make your Japanese interlocutor uncomfortable. The best way for them to avoid that scenario is to disappear from plain sight and go incommunicado permanently.

The avoidance of unpleasantness, embarrassment, difficulties, awkward moments, etc. has been drilled into everyone here from birth. So, being a little fast and loose with the truth is felt to be a much better idea than flagrant confrontation. In the West, we are very ideological about the truth. Japan, less so.

What can you do about it? Nothing. This is the culture and your muscular beliefs on how Japan should be run are every enlightening. We thank you for your contribution to society, but things are not going to change around here. Ever.

In some ways, we have to become temporarily deaf. People who lose their hearing have to compensate with their eyes. They become highly adept at understanding what is going on by watching the body language of the other party. We should stop relying too much on what we are being told verbally. We should be fully focused on reading the smallest indications of resistance in their body language. We need to do this while they are still captive in the meeting room, before they have time to escape. We need to dig deeper into what we can sense will be a difficult decision for them to agree to. This is the time to be frank and get a better read on the likely outcome.

Make it easy for them. Say, "Suzuki-san, I understand that there will be a series of internal processes involved to agree to my proposal. I know you will support me, so thank you for that, but, realistically, do you think this is going to be difficult internally?" Side note here: the English word "difficult" is normally translated into Japanese as *muzukashii*. This is, in fact, a poor translation. The real nuance in business is closer to "impossible" rather than "difficult". So, when you ask this question, the Japanese person is hearing, "Isn't this going to be impossible internally?" They are likely to say, "Yes, it will be *muzukashii*". You know right there and then that your proposal is a dead duck.

In my first business meeting in Japan, I remember that the people I was meeting told me they would *maemuki ni kento itashimasu*—they would study my proposal in a positive light. I was so excited, because I thought I had landed my first deal in Japan.

A more experienced Japan hand wised me up when he said that answer was code for "No". This was my first encounter with *tatemae* and *honne*—the public face and the real face of Japan. Nothing has changed 40 years later!

In the final chapter, we will look at why Japan is a graveyard for change agent leaders.

36—Japan Is a Graveyard for Change Agent Leaders

Your firm's Japan business has been around for many years, but it never seems to live up to expectations. An aging Japanese CEO was chosen to head things up, the thinking being, "A Japanese person is the obvious one to lead the business in Japan". It seemed logical at the time, and the individual had many years of experience in the industry.

Sounds good, right? Well, eventually, the penny drops that this very expensive CEO is not much of a leader and isn't up to the task. They can't take on the market and win in Japan. This is where you come in. You are selected for the Tokyo assignment and are honoured to have been picked. So, off you go, bringing the family to this exciting country.

You don't speak the language, so you have trouble directly discussing issues with the staff. But with your assistant doubling as your interpreter, off you go to change the world. Headquarters keeps reminding you that they expect you to get the business to start performing, after many years of it going absolutely nowhere. You don't know what to change at first, so you take some time to understand the lay of the land, the people, clients, market, competitors, etc.

Gradually, it dawns on you that the sales team are not doing a good enough job. They only like seeing the same clients and make no great efforts to source new clients. You also start to realise that your leader group are not much good at leading. They have made it to these positions through dint of age and stage, and haven't had any real leadership training. You start to suggest some things you think will spark more sales. You immediately run into heavy resistance. You are told that you don't understand Japan and things can't change very easily here. It would be better to keep doing what we have always done, the leaders say. You also notice that people are guarded with you and won't open up.

As you get to know Japan better—and speak with more-experienced expats who run businesses here—you start to doubt what you are being told. You also doubt the people telling you. You start to think that the only way to change the business—and get it out of the rut it has fallen into—is to change the people. Meanwhile, headquarters are saying rude things like, "You have been there for nine months and there has been no change in results". They want to know when you are going to get things moving in Japan. You try to explain that Japan is "different", but they have no idea what you are talking about. Your pleas fall on deaf ears.

The results of the global engagement survey come out and Asia–Pacific is the worst-performing region in the world. Japan is the region's worst-performing country. Headquarters want to know why you are not getting the team properly engaged in their work and how you are going to lift these engagement numbers. They expect to see a big improvement by the time of the next survey—or else!

You feel the pressure and realise you have to make major changes, or else you will be sacked. The kids have settled into their new school, and you don't want to uproot the family and head back home in failure. So, you try to fire some of the people who are non-performers, blockers, deadwood. Immediately, you are told by the local HR that you can't fire people in Japan. They will have to stay.

Digging a bit deeper, you realise that you actually can fire people, although the cost of paying them out is considerable. But you bite the bullet on the money and fire them. You bring in new blood, hoping to spruce up the team. The new people are a disappointment, too, and seem to have decided they would rather fit in with the existing team than join the revolution. You couldn't afford to hire A players, so you had to go with B and C players. The new people quickly realise that you will leave after a few years, but they will have to continue to work with their new colleagues. They decide to assimilate with the existing culture and not join your revolution.

You suddenly get an angry call from your boss back at headquarters. "What are you doing over there in Japan?" he wants to know. "The board has received a series of handwritten, unsigned letters from members of staff complaining about you. They are being told you are lazy, incompetent, don't understand Japan, are ruining the brand, and are destroying relationships with clients. And you are sexually harassing the staff". Your boss has been given the task of dealing with this by the board, and they are taking the accusations very seriously—especially the sexual harassment claims. You are astonished and protest your innocence to no great avail.

Your breath is literally taken away by these accusations. Your body is trembling. Who would write such a bunch of blatant lies about you? You start thinking through the members of the team and try to figure out who these assassins are. Everyone shows you respect. They don't openly display any hostility toward you. It is so puzzling. You ask for copies of the letters and have some handwriting experts help you to identify the perpetrators of this massive injustice. Unhelpfully, no clear conclusions can be reached, so you are still in the dark about who is moving against you from within.

Your boss, feeling pressure from the board, is mainly worried about his own backside. He wants to know what you are going to do to fix the mess you have created. You try to explain Japan and how it works, but you realise he is just not listening. To you, it feels like they all seem to think Japan should operate like back at home. You have no support locally, and no air cover back at headquarters. Your rivals back there are having a field day with your troubles and are taking advantage of the situation to push themselves forward as future leaders, instead of you. Your wife expects you to fix it, too, because the kids have made friends at school, she has formed a nice support group for herself, and she doesn't want any disruption to the family unit.

The latest engagement survey has been delivered, and the results are even worse than the previous one. Again, the pressure from headquarters becomes intense. Your mind is in a fog. If you try to incorporate the changes you know need to be made, various local staff will be threatened and will knife you in the back. They have strongly vested interests in seeing things stay just as they were.

Further, they have no compunction and no moral restraints against doing anything to get rid of you, to stop the process of change. They know they can outlast you. All they have to do is freeze the results by doing nothing differently, keep up the pressure, and wait. The letters keep turning up and your boss is on the phone again. But this time you feel a cold, non-supportive attitude and clearly no tolerance for more of the same.

You have been in Japan for a couple of years now and you know better how things work. You now know that most of what your people have been telling you is not true. They say changes can't be made, but what they really mean is that they don't want to make the changes. Well, except one: changing you as the local president.

Finally, your boss calls you and tells you that your assignment has been terminated. You have to return to headquarters. Your wife is very unhappy, because you have to pull the kids out of school. She asks you how you will find a place for the kids in a decent school back home at this stage of the school year. You are utterly defeated by your team, who are silently smirking and triumphant. The door slams hard behind you. In a few weeks, your replacement turns up walks through that same door and round two gets under way. Your assistant quits because her protector has been removed and she can't deal with the team on her own. The score is: Locals 1, Expats 0.

The moral of the story is, if you want to be a change agent in Japan, be very, very careful.

First of all, understand there are absolutely no rules here. This is a vicious, brutal street fight with only one winner, and the odds are stacked against you from day one. Before you even accept the assignment, get guarantees written in blood by the hierarchy at headquarters that you will get air cover once you start making changes and begin to upset the deeply entrenched vested interests in Japan.

Tell them that they can expect unsigned letters accusing you of anything and everything in an attempt to discredit you. Instead of being alarmed, they should see this as an indicator of progress. It means you are making substantive changes for the good of the business. They should ignore them entirely and count them as a cost of change. They have to understand this is a rear-guard action by a bunch of loser holdouts who do not have the firm's best interests at heart. These people will stop at nothing to maintain their cushy positions.

Have the leadership accept that this change process will not succeed in just one or two years. This is major corporate cancer surgery and will have to be sustained over time if the business is to be saved. Get them to agree to a fund for staffing payouts in Japan as you start to cut the deadwood and replace it. Also, get monies put aside to work with head-hunters to source higher-quality A-player leaders who will support what you are doing. You need your own loyal crew in there to help you drive the change and switch the odds in your favour. You want people who are equally committed to change to do the heavy lifting with you. Ask that no engagement surveys be conducted in Japan for five years, because that is how long it will take to see the results of the changes.

Once you get these agreements in place, then take the assignment. If they don't go for it, then decline to go to Japan. You will only face massive stress, sleepless nights, family disruption, and it will leave a nasty stain on your until-now-excellent and unblemished work record. Let some other ambitious executive go and try. Wish them luck. They will need it.

Conclusion

I have covered 36 topics in this book. I am sure we could cover another 136 quite easily. I have tried to focus on topics that will be of the most interest to readers. Japan changes very quickly … and also very slowly. This is one of the many conundrums about doing business in this country. My topic selection was aimed at those issues where change is not so rapid. These are enduring challenges that we face here, and will continue to face forever.

Here is something that I always believe: "If you can make it here, you can make it anywhere". I know Frank Sinatra and New York have the song, but there is something special about business in Tokyo—in Japan—that is not replicated elsewhere. The pickiness of the Japanese consumer, the long-term orientation of the business partners, the high levels of polite service backed up by attention to detail, consistency, loyalty, and precision are special.

We can all learn a lot from Japan about service and reliability. "Going the extra mile" is an English expression, but I bet the concept was invented here, hundreds of years ago. When we master doing business here, we are fully equipped to succeed in business anywhere. Nowhere can be harder than Japan.

This is a safe, well-organized society based on mutual interdependence and respect. Young kids aged six years and up travel to school by train on their own. No one thinks anything about it, because it is not considered to be exceptional. Age and experience are still valued here. Drugs, crime, mass shootings, urban grittiness, litter, graffiti, and personal safety are not major issues in Japan as they are elsewhere. Everything works. You can get the best of the world here—as long as you have enough money to afford it. Everything is design, from the humblest table arrangements for your chopstick holders at lunch to the tallest, most modern skyscrapers.

Is it perfect? Well, no. There are many frustrations in business, which I mentioned in the various chapters. Am I an uncritical observer of things here in Japan, an apologist? No.

On balance, though, this is a great country and a great place to do business—if you know what you are doing. So, I hope this book has helped you reduce some of the friction. I also hope it has helped make you more successful. If that is the case, then the whole exercise has been worthwhile.

Best wishes for great success in Japan.

If you would like to be kept up to date with business in Japan, you might enjoy my weekly podcasts: The Leadership Japan Series, The Sales Japan Series, and The Presentations Japan Series. Also, every Tuesday, I release the latest episode of the *Cutting Edge Japan Business Show* on YouTube.

Dr Greg Story
President, Dale Carnegie Training Japan

greg.story@dalecarnegie.com
enjapan.dalecarnegie.com

About the Author

Dr Greg Story is a sixth-generation Australian born in Brisbane, Queensland. His first job after high school was selling Encyclopædia Britannica door to door. He was a total failure in sales. After four years of working in various "dirty, dangerous, and difficult" jobs, he saved enough money to put himself through university.

Graduating with honours in Modern Asian Studies at Griffith University, he came to Japan in 1979 on a scholarship from the Japanese Ministry of Education, Science and Culture. During that first four-year tour, he began the study of Japanese and completed a Master's Degree at Jochi University in Tokyo. He returned in 1984 to begin field work for his doctorate as a Japan Foundation Fellow. He was later awarded his PhD from Griffith University in Queensland.

After establishing his own consulting business—the Japan Business Consultancy—he resumed his sales career. In 1989, he was recruited by Jones Lang Wootton in Brisbane to run their Japan Desk, selling office buildings, shopping malls, five-star hotels, and golf courses to Japanese corporates.

In 1992, he returned to Japan with the Australian Trade and Investment Commission (Austrade) to establish a startup sales operation in Nagoya. In 1996, he took over Austrade Osaka and, in 2001, he ran Austrade Tokyo, later becoming country head for Austrade in Japan.

In 2003, he joined the Shinsei Retail Bank with instructions to turn around the sales team, which was tasked with selling investment products to wealthy Japanese individuals. In 2007, he became country head for the National Australia Bank in Japan, again focused on financial investment products.

In that same year, he and his partners bought the franchise rights for Dale Carnegie Training in Japan. In 2010, he left the National Australia Bank to work in the Dale Carnegie Training business as its Japan president. In April 2018, he published the bestseller Japan Sales Mastery, the first book on the subject in 30 years.

He is a sixth dan in traditional shitoryu karate. This is his 48th year of karate training, during which time he has been an international athlete, coach, referee, and official. His other great sporting passion is rugby, and he supports the Brisbane Broncos, the Queensland State of Origin Team, the Kangaroos, the Queensland Reds, and the Wallabies.

High-Impact Presentation Course

What Does This Course Deliver?

Teach you how to be a star!

How Does It Do That?

It triggers five major shifts in your presentation's approach

- Builds Massive Self Belief & Confidence
- Achieve Incredible Levels Of Persuasive Power
- Become The Speaker Everyone Wants To Hear Again
- Combine Quality Content With Unmatched Delivery Skills
- Own The Room

Course Availability

It is running all the time
Delivered in Japanese and English

Dale Carnegie Training Japan

TEL: 0120-987-099, 03-4563-1963 weekdays 9:00–18:00, closed Sat/Sun/Holidays

FAX: 03-4563-1964

ENJAPAN.DALECARNEGIE.COM

Winning With Relationship Selling

What Does This Course Deliver?

Teach you how to become a "shoot the lights out" <u>sales professional</u>

How Does It Do That?
It triggers five major shifts in your sales approach

- Build Real Belief In Yourself

- Become Major Value For Your Buyers

- Master Consultative Selling

- Create Client Loyalty & Lifetime Value

- Produce <u>Big Numbers</u>

Course Availability

It is running all the time
Delivered in Japanese and English

Dale Carnegie Training Japan

TEL: 0120-987-099, 03-4563-1963 weekdays 9:00–18:00, closed Sat/Sun/Holidays

FAX: 03-4563-1964

ENJAPAN.DALECARNEGIE.COM

Step Up To Leadership Course

The transition from doing to leading can be tricky because the skill sets are different. Being in charge of oneself and being in charge of others is another level of complexity. The risk is being promoted because you are good at your job and then getting into trouble, because you are not good enough in your new job as a leader.

Step Up To Leadership concentrates on the four key skills needed to make this transition from doing to leading:

- Getting clarity about what is the role of a leader and what is different to being a member of staff
- Becoming an effective communicator who is clear, concise and motivational
- Coaching at a professional level, getting the highest possible performance in the team
- Using Performance Management skills to make sure the targets are being achieved

This programme will help you to become a successful and confident leader.

Course Availability
It is running all the time
Delivered in Japanese and English

Dale Carnegie Training Japan

TEL: 0120-987-099, 03-4563-1963 weekdays 9:00–18:00, closed Sat/Sun/Holidays

FAX: 03-4563-1964

ENJAPAN.DALECARNEGIE.COM

Leadership Training For Managers

What Does This Course Deliver?

Teach you how to become the leader people <u>want to follow</u>

How Does It Do That?

It triggers five major shifts in your leadership

- Create Your Personal Leadership Sweet Spot
- Achieve Massive Leverage Through Your Team
- Produce Super Innovation
- Build "Crawl Over Broken Glass" Loyal Followers
- Drive Consistently <u>Big Results</u>

Course Availability

It is running all the time
Delivered in Japanese and English

Dale Carnegie Training Japan

TEL: 0120-987-099, 03-4563-1963 weekdays 9:00–18:00, closed Sat/Sun/Holidays

FAX: 03-4563-1964

ENJAPAN.DALECARNEGIE.COM

Successful Public Speaking Course

When you are not skilled, speaking in front of others is stressful. When we are the presenter, we are carrying the twin burdens of personal and company brands on our shoulders. How to construct and how to deliver a speech are both skill sets we can learn. We are not born with these abilities, we all learn them. The higher we climb in our responsibilities the quicker we will be called upon to speak to groups, both internally and externally.

The Successful Public Speaking Course teaches the following practical steps:
- How to design an opening that breaks through all the noise and grabs the attention of your audience
- How to design the main body of the talk that delivers the evidence to get the audience agreeing with you
- How to be in total control no matter how ferocious and difficult the Q&A
- How to prepare two closes — one for before and one for after Q&A, that resonate with your audience

You will get real practice with tremendous amounts of coaching to see you soar as a speaker.

Course Availability
It is running all the time
Delivered in Japanese and English

Dale Carnegie Training Japan

TEL: 0120-987-099, 03-4563-1963 weekdays 9:00–18:00, closed Sat/Sun/Holidays

FAX: 03-4563-1964

ENJAPAN.DALECARNEGIE.COM

Confident English Course

Speaking English and speaking up in English are not the same thing. Many Japanese people study English but are shy to speak up in meetings. Not being able to speak and not speaking have the same result — you become invisible in international meetings.

The Confident English Course teaches these key skills:
- Overcome being held back by an obsession with having to be perfect in English
- Learn how to raise your hand and ask a question and have people listen to you
- Be able to put forward your own opinion on a topic in the meeting and be taken seriously
- Have the confidence to differ with the speaker's opinion and explain why
- Make rapid and lasting progress in writing and speaking in English

Course Availability
It is running all the time
Delivered in Japanese and English

Dale Carnegie Training Japan

TEL: 0120-987-099, 03-4563-1963 weekdays 9:00–18:00, closed Sat/Sun/Holidays

FAX: 03-4563-1964

ENJAPAN.DALECARNEGIE.COM

The Cutting Edge Japan Business Show
with Dr. Greg Story

This is THE premier business show in Japan.

We cover the all key topics of most value for you to succeed here.

Don't try and figure it out by yourself using trial and error – that is definitely the hard way to do things in Japan.

Based on over thirty years of hard won experience in Japan, Dr. Greg Story, Your Corporate Coaching and Training Guy, takes you through the short cuts on how to succeed in Japan.

Watch The Cutting Edge Japan Business Show every week, released Tuesdays on YouTube, to gain key knowledge about doing business in Japan.

If you prefer to listen to podcasts, then listen to The Cutting Edge Japan Business Show podcast version every week, where ever you get your podcasts.

Dale Carnegie Training Japan

TEL: 0120-987-099, 03-4563-1963 / FAX: 03-4563-1964

weekdays 9:00–18:00, closed Sat/Sun/Holidays

ENJAPAN.DALECARNEGIE.COM

The Japan Business Mastery Show

with Dr. Greg Story

In this show we provide the quick grabs of key information about business in Japan, that busy, busy businesspeople need.

Save time and get the best insights.

Watch The Japan Business Mastery Show every week, released Fridays on YouTube, to ramp up your business success.

If you prefer podcasts, then listen to The Japan Business Mastery Show podcast version every week, where ever you get your podcasts.

Dale Carnegie Training Japan

TEL: 0120-987-099, 03-4563-1963

FAX: 03-4563-1964

weekdays 9:00–18:00, closed Sat/Sun/Holidays

ENJAPAN.DALECARNEGIE.COM

The Sales Japan Series

with Dr. Greg Story

Understanding the buyer is critical to
sales success in Japan.

It is so easy to make it hard for yourself.

Don't do it that way.

The Sales Japan Series podcast pulls back
the velvet curtain on how to sell in Japan.

Listen to the Sales Japan Series podcast and
save yourself a lot of time, money and tears.

Dale Carnegie Training Japan

TEL: 0120-987-099, 03-4563-1963

FAX: 03-4563-1964

weekdays 9:00–18:00, closed Sat/Sun/Holidays

ENJAPAN.DALECARNEGIE.COM

The Leadership Japan Series
with Dr. Greg Story

Leading in Japan is different.

As we have all found, it has its own special challenges.

Don't try and figure it out all by yourself.

Short circuit the whole process.

Listen to The Leadership Japan Series podcast episodes for the best information on leading in Japan.

Dale Carnegie Training Japan

TEL: 0120-987-099, 03-4563-1963

FAX: 03-4563-1964

weekdays 9:00–18:00, closed Sat/Sun/Holidays

ENJAPAN.DALECARNEGIE.COM

The Presentations Japan Series

with Dr. Greg Story

There is no doubt that the ability to present well is a game changer in business.

Be it to clients, colleagues, senior executives, shareholders or industry peers, these are always make or break occasions when you are presenting.

Remember, this is your personal and professional brand on the line here – don't blow it.

Listen to the Presentations Japan Series podcasts to learn all the secrets to becoming a great presenter.

Dale Carnegie Training Japan

TEL: 0120-987-099, 03-4563-1963

FAX: 03-4563-1964

weekdays 9:00–18:00, closed Sat/Sun/Holidays

ENJAPAN.DALECARNEGIE.COM

Dale Carnegie Course®

Effective Communications & Human Relations

What Does This Course Deliver?

This course will <u>change your life</u> and produce a new and much improved you!

How Does It Do That?

It triggers five major shifts in your life

- Become Super Confident
- Ace Your Communication
- Become A Real Leader
- Obtain Awesome People Skills
- Totally Control Your Stress

Course Availability

It is running all the time
Delivered in Japanese and English

Dale Carnegie Training Japan

TEL: 0120-987-099, 03-4563-1963 weekdays 9:00–18:00, closed Sat/Sun/Holidays

FAX: 03-4563-1964

ENJAPAN.DALECARNEGIE.COM

Dale Carnegie

Made in the USA
Lexington, KY
02 December 2019